The Theory and Practice of Human Rights

The Theory and Practice of Human Rights

L.J. MACFARLANE

ST. MARTIN'S PRESS
NEW YORK

First published in the United States of America in 1985
All rights reserved. For information, write:
St. Martin's Press, Inc., 175 Fifth Avenue, New York, NY 10010

ISBN 0-312-79716-8

Library of Congress Cataloging in Publication Data
Macfarlane, L. J. (Leslie John), 1924-
  The Theory and Practice of Human Rights.

  Includes index.
  1. Civil rights. I. Title.
JC571.M2132 1985   323.4   84-27743
ISBN 0-312-79716-8

Typeset in Times, 10pt 2pt leaded by Tellgate Ltd., 27 Swinton Street,
London WC1 1DB
Printed in Great Britain by The Camelot Press, Southampton

Contents

To Rebecca

Preface

Man is born endowed with universally acclaimed human rights, but everywhere such rights are violated or ignored. *Amnesty International Report 1983* identifies human rights abuses in more than one hundred and fifteen countries, 'many . . . committed by governments whose own officials pay lip-service to human rights in international arenas such as the United Nations.'[1] But while the standard official response to alleged violations is a blunt denial or a counter-allegation of misrepresentation, in private more plausible reasons or explanations may be offered. Thus it is claimed that many countries find themselves in the position of being required by international opinion to endorse United Nations human rights declarations and covenants (since to refuse to do so is to label oneself as an enemy of human rights), even though social divisiveness and political instability, coupled with a deficient institutional framework and inadequate resources, make it impossible adequately to comply with the requirements accepted. Alternatively it is argued either that the human rights laid down by the United Nations are so vaguely defined as to make it impossible to establish what constitutes a rights violation, or that they require to be interpreted by reference to the particular values and traditions of each particular society. It is very much with these considerations in mind that this book has been written.

It opens with an examination of the problems inherent in using the accepted defining characteristics of human rights as criteria capable of being strictly applied to verify whether any claimed right should be accorded human right status, or to determine whether a particular country has given effect to a right so established. In the light of this analysis subsequent chapters discuss selected key rights with a view to determining what minimum area and practical form of the right can be substantiated in universally applicable terms. The book closes with a review of the issues involved in securing the implementation of validated human rights in a divided world of nation states each with its own distinctive culture and social environment.

I am grateful for the help and advice given by my colleague Dr M.H. Mendelson, international lawyer, and for the ever-present assistance of my wife. The book is dedicated to my grand-daughter, Rebecca, in the hope, but not alas the expectation, that she and her generation 'in all the lands may live out their lives in freedom from fear and want' – Atlantic Charter declaration by President Franklin D. Roosevelt and Prime Minister Winston Churchill, 14 August 1941.

L.J. Macfarlane

St John's College, Oxford
June 1984

1

The Nature of Human Rights

Human rights are those moral rights which are owed to each man or woman by every man or woman solely by reason of being human. Human rights are distinguished from other moral rights in possessing the following inherent characteristics:

    (i)   universality
   (ii)   individuality
 (iii)   paramountcy
 (iv)   practicability
  (v)   enforceability

(i) Universality

Maurice Cranston in *What are Human Rights?* has asserted that human rights differ from other moral rights 'in being the rights of all people at all times and in all situations'.[1] But it is only in terms of our present conceptions and values that we can ascribe moral rights to past persons and peoples who lack any notion of rights. What has to be recognized is that the concept of universal human rights embodies values which not only conflict with other strongly held values and conceptions, but which are incompatible with, and subversive of, certain forms of society and social institutions. Professor Milne has seen the paradoxical implications of this in the United Nations Universal Declaration of Human Rights which 'professes to be a statement of human rights, irrespective of the particular social and political order under which they happen to live', but which 'goes on to enumerate a detailed list of rights which presupposes the values and institutions of a certain kind of social and political order, namely liberal democratic, industrial society.'[2] Professor Milne's solution to the paradox is to scrap the Universal Declaration and to substitute his own list of six basic human rights which all men owe to their fellows – to life, to respect for one's dignity as a person, to be dealt with honestly, to have one's interests fairly considered, to be free from arbitrary coercion and interference, to have one's distress relieved. These basic rights are to be understood and implemented in ways appropriate to the values and institutions of the particular community concerned; though he notes that certain values and institutions are incompatible with any conception of universal moral rights. Only on this basis, Professor Milne argues, can the idea of human rights be given significance for Third World and Communist states – a significance to which these states are entitled, since it *is* possible for the members of such societies to live together as fellow human beings. Nevertheless he accepts that there is a case for requiring all nations to be constitutional states, subject to the rule of law and with legal safeguards against racial discrimination.[3]

The qualifications which Professor Milne introduces are highly significant, since they mean that Governments are not entitled to apply human rights principles as they think fit, according to the needs and requirements of their own system, where this involves discrimination or disregard for constitutional legality and the rule of law. For it is precisely these charges which figure most prominently in the indictment of the sorely pressed Human Rights organizations of the Communist states against their own governments. It is misleading to present the Universal Declaration of Human Rights as though it imposed alien Western liberal democratic values on the rest of the international community. On the contrary these other countries by their voluntary ratification of the International Covenants on Civil and Political Rights and on Economic, Social and Cultural Rights helped bring these Covenants into force. The Soviet Union by its adoption at the Helsinki Conference in 1975 of a Declaration proclaiming 'the right of the individual to know and act upon his rights and duties in this field' (of human rights and fundamental freedoms), helped promote the creation of Helsinki Monitor groups in the USSR. What is striking is that it is precisely the civil and political rights, characterized by Professor Milne as narrowly liberal democratic, which arouse the greatest enthusiasm among the peoples of the Communist states when given the opportunity to express themselves, as in Czechoslovakia in 1968 and Poland in 1980-81. The civil and political rights set out in the

Universal Declaration and the International Covenant are rights which have secured such universal support and approval that the Governments of virtually all states feel compelled to give at least nominal adherence. Far from being rights relevant only to the minority of the world's peoples who live in liberal democratic states, they are seen as of universal concern. Rights, such as the right to freedom of expression and association, are not only vital to the concept of living as full human beings one with another, but are necessary means for securing and protecting all other human rights. The universal character of a human right is to be determined by whether all men require it if they are to live as full human beings, not by whether its realization and enjoyment is compatible with the continued existence of particular forms of society, whether past or present.

The concept of human rights emerged out of the much earlier conception of natural right, which initially was no more than a derivative element in the medieval Christian doctrine of Natural Law. Natural rights were the moral expectations men had that others should behave towards them in accordance with the requirements of Natural Law. At the beginning of the seventeenth century Hugo Grotius gave a new force and direction to the concept by producing a strong theory of natural right as a foundation for political discourse and political understanding, instead of as a mere derivative of Natural Law. This found expression, as Richard Tuck has shown, in both a conservative and a radical theory of natural rights: the former emphasizing the alienation of rights inherent in the formation of civil society (as in Hobbes), the latter the right of resistance to tyranny (as in Locke).[4] More importantly, for our purpose, the radical theory of natural rights was taken up in the seventeenth century by a political movement, the Levellers, and used as the basis for a populist political programme. Natural rights as the rights which all men were entitled to have vouchsafed to them became, in the political market place of the Army Debates, claims against established authority, established institutions and established government. Rainborough's bold assertion 'that the poorest he that is in England hath a life to live, as the greatest he',[5] was seen by the Puritan Army leaders as a challenge to their political authority and to their social position as property holders. Whatever one may think of the force of the particular rights claims of the Levellers, (which embraced economic and social, as well as political and civil, rights), one has to recognize that universal claims made in the name of all are often in practice claims on behalf of the existing deprived against more fortunate minorities to surrender their privileges. Claims to universal rights must be seen as claims to which one can establish a universal entitlement, rather than claims which have universal support. Universal rights necessarily preclude any discrimination or exclusion, whether on grounds of 'race, colour, sex, language, religion, political or other opinion, national or social origin, property, birth or other status'.[6]

The criterion of universality is questioned by Raymond Plant on the grounds that a strict application would rule out all claimants other than the right to life, since all other rights are rights necessarily limited to some people only, while if loosely applied to all those rights which men are capable of exercising, or are liable to find themselves needing to exercise, the bounds are limitless. But it is misleading to argue, as Plant does, that the rights to a fair trial, to leave one's country, to freedom of religion and assembly, are rights 'restricted to those who belong to the particular group in question'.[7] The right to a fair trial is not a right 'necessarily' limited to those persons who are on trial at any particular point in time, but is a positive expression of the liberty right of all men not to be subject at any time to arbitrary arrest, imprisonment or punishment. The right to leave and return to one's country is not a right vested in those who wish to do so, but a particular aspect of the right of all members of a political community to freedom of movement, i.e. a right not to be hindered or prevented by others from moving freely. The right to freedom of worship is a right of all men not to be interfered with in the practice of their Faith or their non-Faith,[8] not a right appertaining only to existing members of particular religious groups. Rights to act, like the right to peaceful assembly, are by their very nature entitlements individuals may or may not wish or choose to exercise. Plant appears to confuse those having a right with those wishing or choosing to exercise it.

(ii) Individuality
The concept of rights is grounded in and derives much of its support and colouring from the acceptance of man as a free individual, a being of dignity and worth, endowed with reason and conscience, and capable of moral choice and free activity. Where that value is not accepted there is no place for rights as of right, but only for rights as of concession or of custom.[9] Human rights are the rights of individuals, to meet the needs and purposes of individuals. But, since some needs and purposes can only be met by individuals acting in concert, it is

necessary to recognize the right of individuals to associate together and the right of the associations so formed to operate freely under the law. Association, however, always involves some restriction of members' freedom of action in relation to each other, restriction which commonly finds expression in rules and through organizational structure. There is thus a potential built-in tension both between individual members of the association and between members and the association as constituted. The problems which arise in this connection are discussed in Chapter 5.

While human rights are the rights of individuals they are first and foremost rights against society rather than against other individuals, since it is society's responsibility to ensure that the rights concerned are given legal force and upheld against all persons and bodies within the community. In modern states this responsibility devolves directly on the Government, imposing in its stead a strict and special obligation not itself to infringe or neglect the rights it has a responsibility to secure. How far other persons and bodies have obligations in respect to rights implementation will depend on the nature of the right concerned. Rights to non-interference are rights against all persons and bodies, whereas rights to economic and social benefits are likely to be, primarily at least, rights against the state. One of the major concerns in the following chapters is to substantiate precisely what obligations are imposed on which particular persons and bodies with respect to specific human rights.

(iii) Paramountcy
Maurice Cranston writes of a human right being 'something of which no one can be deprived without a grave affront to justice. There are certain deeds which should never be done, certain freedoms which should never be invaded, some things which are supremely sacred.' He admits, however, the difficulty of providing a definitive criterion of paramountcy.[10] One answer has been provided by Professor Dworkin in the distinction he draws between weak and strong moral rights; where the latter are those rights which it would be wrong for a Government to override simply on the grounds that the exercise of the right is not in the public interest, or is contrary to the majority will. Such strong moral rights are paramount in that individuals are, where necessary, entitled to exercise them in spite of law to the contrary. That is not to say that strong rights may never be legally overriden, or the law enforced against those asserting strong rights; but that such

overriding action can be justified only if one of the following conditions is met:

(i) the strong right asserted conflicts with laws which the citizen would have a right to have enacted if they were not already law, (e.g. right to protection against personal physical assault);

(ii) the strong right is legally overriden by the government in time of emergency, where a 'clear and present danger' of great magnitude can be objectively established: a danger which can be overcome only if that right is put in cold storage for the duration of the emergency, (with guarantees of its resuscitation);

(iii) a particular claimed instance can be shown to lie outside the limits of the established strong rights area, because:

  (a) the values protected by the established strong right are not really at stake in the marginal case, or at stake only in an attenuated form; or

  (b) if the right is defined to include the marginal case then some competing strong right would be abridged in some serious respect; or

  (c) if the right is defined to include the marginal case the extra cost to society would not be simply incremental but of such a magnitude as to justify whatever restrictions are involved.[11]

Within the context of a country such as the United States the concept of strong rights may be used, as Dworkin does, to extend the present area of individual freedom to the maximum consistent with avoiding collapse of society. Such a maximum, however, could never be an international minimum. On the contrary paramount universal human rights are those minimum strong moral rights of which no man or woman may be deprived by Government or society whether by arbitrary fiat or by law. In these terms it will be possible to provide for local variations in the form in which particular minimum area rights are established in societies differing widely in culture and in structure, and to allow for local action designed to secure domestic rights space beyond the minimum encapsulated in the universal human right.

But can the concept of paramountcy be applied to economic and social rights or are they, as Cranston suggests, excluded as rights of a different degree of moral urgency?[12] Cranston himself, unwittingly, provides strong grounds for rejecting this conclusion in his acceptance 'of a paramount duty to relieve great distress'.[13] There can be no doubt that amongst the poor, especially the poor majority in the Third World, great distress derives primarily from economic and social, rather than from civil and political, causes.

This approach finds clear expression in Raymond Plant's assertion that one can derive a paramountcy criterion from the concept of basic human needs which must be met if men are to pursue any of the possible variety of goals embodied in any universalizable moral code. Plant identifies two basic human needs which all societies ought to acknowledge a moral responsibility to provide: the need for survival and the need for moral autonomy. From these he deduces fundamental social needs in the areas of health, education and welfare, giving rise to minimum rights to services and benefits which societies are under a strict obligation to fulfil. Plant recognizes that the relevant minimum will vary from society to society and from one period to another. He charts the more crucial difficulties inherent in establishing valid criteria of need, having regard both to the different perceptions of welfare recipients and welfare workers, the different conceptions of social needs to be found in different moral and social theories, and conflicting ideas as to how far such needs should be met by society or by individuals themselves.[14] Though Plant succeeds, in my view, in establishing a substantial case for the principle of basic human welfare rights grounded in needs, the crucial question remains of whether it is possible to establish specific economic and social rights claims capable of being given effect to in legislation. More particularly this approach fails to come to grips with the question of the rights of those in poor countries which lack the resources for minimum rights provision, a problem discussed in Chapter 8.

(iv) Practicability

The assertion that one cannot have a right to the impossible has been all too readily used as an argument against the whole area of social and economic rights. Human rights claims are, of course, never made to what is physically impossible (to live forever), or to what must necessarily be restricted to a very small minority (to have one's own personal and exclusive private physician); nor are they made in terms of what is now enjoyable by only a small minority of the world's population. Thus, the poor of the Third World claim the right to an adequate livelihood, not the right to live as well as the average man of the Western world. What cannot be accepted in the name of practicability is that the most that men can have a right to is what their own civil society, as at present organized, can provide for all its inhabitants; since even to meet the minimum basic needs of the population may require substantial changes in its established institutions and practices, involving restrictions on the privileges and powers of existing elites. Practicability has rather to be established in terms of the probability that proposed changes will help meet the basic economic and social needs of the poor with the minimum disturbance of existing rights and customary ways.

Practicability is an issue with all human rights, not just economic and social rights, since resources are always required either for their realization or their protection. But whereas with economic and social rights the resources devoted to buildings, equipment and personnel are required to provide a direct service, in the case of traditional liberty rights they are required to protect persons against interference with their rights. Once adequate resources have been provided economic and social rights can be secured, but this is not true of liberty rights, since no matter what the level of resources devoted to protection there will always be transgressions of rights to non-interference. Indeed in the modern world of urban sprawl and growth, the forces of law and order are less and less able to provide an adequate measure of protection of the public from violence and crime.

The right to free primary education for all is a clearly defined right which each parent has for his or her own children – a right which can be 'cashed in' at the local school. The right to protection from physical violence, on the other hand, is much less specific both in the sense of being much less clearly defined, and in the sense of not being afforded to each person as an individual ration. In consequence while it might be argued that nobody in New York City or Chicago is effectively protected against muggers and hoodlums on the streets, this would not in itself appear to justify an assertion that the authorities were denying citizens their rights of protection. Indeed it is not readily apparent what general level of protection can reasonably be expected or required of such authorities. Even if one could establish the level and form of protection which authorities were required to provide, based on the minimum protection entitlements of a citizen, it would still not be possible for each and every individual citizen to require that he be secured that specified degree of protection. Still less would it be possible actually to secure him from any invasion of his protection rights. The notion of a right to a minimum level of protection for each citizen, unlike the right to a minimum level of education for each child, does not lend itself to expression in terms of individual entitlements, but only in terms of social obligations to provide a level of service to the community based on average requirements. It must, therefore, be accepted that the right to protection underpinning all liberty rights is neither a right which can be fully secured nor a right vested in individuals.

(v) Enforceability

The issue of international enforceability of human rights is a much more complex one than it appears to Maurice Cranston, who writes 'There is nothing essentially difficult about transforming political and civil rights into positive rights. All that is needed is an international court with real powers of enforcement.'[15] International Courts are not capable of carrying out the role which Cranston would assign to them. Even the European Court of Justice of the European Economic Community (EEC) relies on member states complying with its rulings in cases involving alleged breaches of obligations under the EEC Treaty. If a member state defies a Court ruling there is no provision under the EEC Treaty, as there is under the European Coal and Steel Community Treaty,[16] for the use of sanctions against the delinquent. When an EEC Member State fails to comply, the matter 'passes outside the realm of the law and becomes political,' resolvable only by concerted political action on the part of the other Governments to secure a political compromise.[17] While there is no provision under the Community Treaties for the expulsion of a defaulting member state it would be politically possible for all the other members to do so. This would, however, require such a major revision of the whole Community structure and cause such major dislocations, that it is difficult to envisage it being even contemplated. The ultimate safeguard against it being necessary is the liberal democratic nature of the states concerned and their adherence to the principle of the Rule of Law.

The European Court, however, deals only marginally with human rights within Community States, since such states as Members of the Council of Europe are bound by the European Convention for the Protection of Human Rights and Fundamental Freedoms.[18] The Convention provides for a European Commission and a European Court of Human Rights to ensure the implementation of the rights specified. Since the provisions of the European Convention constitute the only effective working system for the legal enforcement of human rights, an examination of its workings will help us to gain an understanding of the problems of human rights enforcement by international bodies.

The first point to note is that the European Convention, which came into force in 1953, has legal force only for those members of the Council of Europe who ratify it.[19] Thus France, though one of the original signatories in 1950, did not ratify the Convention until 1974 and was therefore not subject to its implementation and enforcement provisions for twenty years. Secondly it is open to any contracting Party to denounce the Convention, as Greece did in 1969 (returning again in 1974 after the fall of the military regime). Thirdly it is left to each Party to decide whether to permit individual complaints by another Party (Article 25) and whether to accept the decisions of the European Court of Human Rights as binding (Article 46). Five states (Cyprus, Greece, Liechtenstein, Malta and Turkey) have not agreed to the former and three (Liechtenstein, Malta and Turkey) to the latter. The Committee of Ministers of the Council of Europe is finally responsible for ensuring that judgements of the Court are given effect to, but its only sanction is that of expulsion from the Council of Europe. The Committee was in the process of considering a proposal to expel Greece in 1969, when Greece got in first by withdrawing from the Council and denouncing the Convention. What this example reveals is the emptiness of this ultimate sanction against an intransigent violating Party, since gross violations of human rights by the military regime continued unabated.

The conclusion which must be drawn is that there is no way in which human rights violations can be redressed by an international court against a State Party determined to brook no interference. Even in a tightly-knit and integrated body like the European Economic Community it may take years to get a European Court decision applied by a resistant member state.[20] It is of the very nature of international legal instruments, as distinct from domestic ones, that the obligations they impose have to be voluntarily assumed by the parties concerned; in particular provisions relating to complaints by individuals against their own government and to the determination and enforcement of breaches of the substantive obligations assumed. As we have seen, even if the provisions of the International Covenant on Civil and Political Rights (ICPR) were brought in line with those of the European Convention on Human Rights, it would still be open to any United Nations member state not to permit individual applications and not to be bound by judicial decisions. That is not to say that a strengthening of the enforcement provisions of United Nations International Covenants is not to be desired, but only to stress that such a strengthening would not, in itself, bring about substantial reductions in human rights violations in violating states. Human rights enforcement is essentially a matter of domestic politics rather than of international law.

HUMAN RIGHTS AS LEGAL RIGHTS

Human rights as enforceable domestic legal rights require a domestic legal system based on the rule of law, affording protection to individuals in the enjoyment of rights under the law with no punishment except for established breaches of the law. What has to be stressed, however, is that the concept of human rights as the legal rights to which all men are entitled under domestic law has a crucial bearing on what constitutes a legal system based on the rule of law.[21] Thus the requirement that 'Everyone shall have the right to recognition everywhere as a person before the law' (ICPR Article 16 – not subject to derogation), has to be understood in terms of Article 21 which requires that all the rights under that Covenant be recognized without distinction or discrimination with regard to 'race, colour, sex, language, religion, political or other opinion, national or social origin, property, birth or other status'. The enforcement of publicly promulgated law by properly constituted and impartial courts is unacceptable if the laws being given effect to are themselves in conflict with human rights requirements.

The rule of law is the antithesis of arbitrary government and is embodied in ICPR (Article 15 – not subject to derogation) as the right not to be held guilty of any criminal offence on account of any act not embodied in law. It is incompatible with this requirement that a statute should be so loosely or ambiguously phrased as to give the political authorities unrestricted discretionary powers. The members of every state have an unqualified right to know what they are not permitted to do and ought not to be left to the doubtful mercies and whims of officials entrusted with the determination of criminality under the rule of licence masquerading as law.

A second requirement of the rule of law is that no one should be subject to detention except under procedures which provide for a fair trial before a public court. Although this right may be derogated 'in time of public emergency which threatens the life of the nation' (ICCPR Article 4.1),[22] the very notion of derogation is incompatible with the permanent retention by the state of an arbitrary power to imprison without trial those persons whom the authorities wish to put quietly out of the way. The security of every citizen is at risk if any citizen is subjected to arbitrary confinement without due process of law.

The characteristics of a fair trial are readily established. Each accused person is entitled to:

> presumption of innocence
> information as to the alleged offence under known and established law
> public trial without undue delay
> right to legal assistance and time to prepare defence
> right to examine witnesses
> right not to be compelled to testify against oneself
> right not to be compelled to confess guilt.

These requirements can be justified in two ways. In the first place it can be argued that the denial of any one of them would seriously weaken the chances of establishing beyond all reasonable doubt whether an accused was guilty or not guilty, and in particular, markedly increase the possibility of an innocent person being wrongfully convicted. Secondly the existence of these fair trial entitlements is something each one of us would wish for ourselves if we were accused of a criminal offence, whether rightfully or wrongfully, but particularly if wrongfully. The requirements which bear most directly and substantially on the liberty and security of the person are the right to a presumption of innocence, the right to be brought to trial without undue delay, the right not to be compelled to testify against oneself and the right not to be forced to confess one's guilt.

With regard to a presumption of innocence the crucial requirement is that the Court should not be predisposed to assume that accused persons are guilty persons. A presumption of guilt undermines the whole concept of a fair trial. Any one of us would be appalled and horrified at the nightmare prospect of being 'tried' as an 'already-guilty' person. Though 'undue delay' is subject to a variety of interpretations and practical applications the principle itself is readily understood, since in the hands of an unscrupulous government detention before trial may readily become detention without trial. Detention before trial is justified only to the extent that time is required to prepare the prosecution case and arrange for a trial to be held. It must not become a substitute for, or preliminary form of, punishment. Unduly long detention before trial is at its most objectionable where it is used by detention authorities to put physical or psychological pressure on a prisoner to extract a confession from him. This procedure was the central feature underlying the Soviet show trials of the nineteen-thirties – a feature which the Soviet prosecutors were understandably concerned to conceal.[23]

The right of the accused not to be compelled to testify against himself is perhaps less obviously an essential requirement of a fair trial; since it might be thought that no innocent man would have reason to fear testifying. Historically the right not to testify against oneself has been strongly associated with the right not to be subject to torture or other pressure in order to secure confession of guilt. Such practices are indefensible and undefended – no political society admits to the use of torture. Universal condemnation of the practice and universal denial of its use by practitioner states serves to substantiate the fundamental nature of the right of the accused not to be physically or psychologically forced to confess. What is less clear is whether one may claim a fundamental right of the accused to refuse to answer incriminating questions or to go into the dock. The former right may be claimable by all witnesses and not just the accused, but the latter by the accused only. In its weaker but more extensive form the claimed right provides protection for witnesses against having to make a forced choice between answering an incriminating question which may lead to prosecution, or to prosecution for refusing to answer the question. Since experience shows that only in an ideal, and therefore unrealizable, legal world would an innocent witness run no risk of prosecution and conviction, the right not to answer incriminating questions serves as an additional protection for innocent witnesses including the defendant; though at the expense of also affording protection to guilty defendants and witnesses guilty of other indictable offences.

A fair trial will only be secured if those who work the system are committed to such a conception and permitted to give effect to it. Its most fundamental requirement is the existence of an independent judiciary and an independent legal profession. If judges and counsel are cyphers of the state, or of some ruling party or *junta*, trials, especially political trials, will be farces moving along rehearsed lines to predetermined finales. Even where judges and counsel are not cyphers they may be subject to pressure or intimidation of such an order or character as to pervert the course of justice. While all states claim to have an independent judiciary, the validity of a claim in any particular state may readily be tested by checking to see how many judgements in cases involving fundamental human rights have been made contrary to the wishes of the prosecution, and what has happened to judges handing down adverse judgements. Both the innocent accused and the guilty unable to subvert the cause of justice would wish to be tried before independent judges not in the hands or pockets of the state; while the present rulers who fix trials and the present judges who oblige them would themselves stand in special need of a fair trial and fair judges if they were ousted from power and tried for their former alleged offences. What is seriously open to question, however, is whether not only the Communist states but other one-party regimes could permit fair trials before independent judges of persons accused of political offences, without putting the future of the political system concerned at serious risk.

Those found guilty of a criminal offence after trial are sentenced to punishment, which in the more serious cases commonly takes the form of imprisonment. While imprisonment necessarily involves a serious loss of personal liberty it does not permit the prisoner to be treated as a rightless person. Though standards and forms of treatment are bound to vary markedly from state to state, there are certain minimum standards which states are morally required to uphold. In the first instance they must never as a matter of deliberate policy seek to subject prisoners, or some categories of prisoner, to cruel, inhuman, or degrading treatment or punishment,[24] or to living conditions or forms of forced labour which undermine their health, their sanity or their personality. The most cruel and sadistic killer, if not executed for committing a capital offence, has the right not to be subjected to punishments as morally depraved as those he had himself inflicted on his victims. To fail to abide by this moral requirement is to reduce society to the level it condemns and seeks to eradicate, to give vent to the most primitive passions for revenge which organized society exists to restrain and replace, and to coarsen and corrupt those state officials whose task it is to inflict such punishment.

Governments have an obligation to take all reasonable steps to ensure that prison officials do not abuse their position to exploit, humiliate, or inflict pain or injury on prisoners. Given the closed form of prison society and the nature of the power relationship, there is always a substantial risk of serious and extensive violations of human rights of security of the person, resulting from aggressive action either by prison staff themselves or from prison staff failing to prevent aggressive action by one prisoner on another. Prisoners sentenced to punishment by the Courts for an offence have a fundamental right not to be subject to further infliction of pain or injury either by the state authorities or other persons: no body or person can have a legal or moral right to inflict such an additional penalty or suffering. To condone such action is to deny the legal principles which lie at the basis of the modern state.

Where fundamental human rights are not enforced in any state those so denied are entitled to take action to secure these rights for themselves, provided that in so doing they do not violate the rights of others. I am entitled to refuse to comply with legal restrictions or legal obligations in clear conflict with fundamental human rights requirements. The right to seek to enforce my rights against a wilfully defaulting state should be seen both as a crucial ingredient of what constitutes a fundamental human right and as a measure by which to determine whether any claimed moral right should be accorded fundamental human right status. It is in this spirit that the Preamble of the Universal Declaration of Human Rights boldly declaims: 'Whereas it is essential, if man is not to be compelled to have recourse, as a last resort, to rebellion against tyranny and oppression, that human rights should be protected by the rule of law.'[25]

2
The Right to Life

There is a very real sense in which all human rights derive from and are dependent on the self-evident nature of the right to life claimed in the American Declaration of Independence. Yet man cannot convincingly demonstrate an unqualified inherent right to live on, still less to exercise dominion over, planet earth: any such claims would doubtless appear immoral to the dolphin and irrational to the Martian. Man's underlying presumptions and beliefs need not, however, be seen as reflecting a human 'false consciousness' as to his own position, lacking any claim to objective meaning or validity. In a physically real if not an absolute sense these beliefs arise out of man's singular capacity as a self-conscious being to understand the world in which he lives – a capacity which could embrace the ability and readiness to carry on a dialogue with dolphins and Martians as to the rights of animals and of alien-beings.

But if man's seemingly unique characteristic of self-conscious creativity can provide a foundation for a claimed right for continued human existence, a basis has been laid for a human right to life; since self-consciousness and creative action, though characteristic of all members of the species, only find expression in and through the diverse activities of individual persons. It is because each individual man or woman is aware of his or her self as a distinct self-directed being with a life to lead and to cherish, that a claim may be made on behalf of each and every human being of a right to live.[1] It is vital at the very outset to stress the radical nature of such a claim, asserting as it does that every person, irrespective of his or her class, colour, sex, religion, nationality, birth or status has a right to life valid against all other persons, which it is the duty of all others to respect and of society to protect.

Though it is universally recognized that all human beings have a 'self-evident' right to life,[2] the precise meaning and practical implications of such a right are not readily apparent and require careful analysis. Whatever else, however, may be involved in the right to life there is agreement that at the core is the right not to be killed or threatened with killing. Since a right needs to be enforceable to be meaningful, any man threatened with death by another has a natural right to defend himself from attack, even if that involves taking the life of his assailant.[3]

Thus at the heart of the right to life there is to be found an apparent fundamental contradiction, a right to kill. It is misleading, however, to interpret the right to defend one's own life from attack either as an assertion of a right to kill the assailant or as a violation of his right to live.[4] The inherent right of self-defence of one's life is not in itself a right to kill, but to use such force as is necessary and available to protect oneself. In attacking me an assailant forfeits his right not to be injured as I seek to defend myself,[5] but he does not forfeit his life to me. If I manage to knock him unconscious I am not then entitled to take his life. If I kill him I may reasonably be required to show that I did so in the course of defending myself, using no more force than was necessary. If I could have temporarily immobilized my assailant with a hypnotic stare I would not have been entitled to use physical force against him. In exactly the same terms I have a right to defend the lives of others from direct murderous assault, or to prevent such assault taking place, by actions which may in the last resort justify my using means which may cause death of the 'would-be' or 'could-be' killer.

What applies to individuals acting in defence of life, in the absence of the forces of law and order, must apply even more directly to those forces themselves when their own lives or the lives of others are threatened in the course of carrying out their proper duties. What is more questionable is whether the police are entitled to shoot at, and possibly kill, criminals, not in self-defence but to prevent their getting away and to do so even in situations where there is a possibility of innocent bystanders being shot. Since, however, it would be difficult to enforce a right of criminals not to be shot at except by requiring the police not to be armed, and since in many countries criminals have guns and are very ready to use them, it would not be reasonable to claim that arming the police constitutes a violation of the right to life, subject to strict conditions being laid down as to the use of arms and with provision for legal accountability.

A different and more hotly contested question is whether the constituted authorities have the right to exact capital punishment on convicted criminals found responsible for the deaths of other persons. This is an issue on which one can readily understand why morally conscientious persons should take up diametrically opposed positions. On the one side it can be argued that, since in a state of nature a man had a right to expect his kith and kin to avenge his murder with the latter recognized as entitled or even obliged to do so, society is entitled, or perhaps required, to uphold the sanctity of life by exacting the death penalty against wilful murderers. On the other side it can be claimed that since life is sacred it may never be deliberately taken as an act of revenge for death, but only risked in defence against a murderous attack. Each of these moral positions appears to meet Professor Hare's criterion of universalizability which 'requires us to choose our final moral judgement or principle *as if* it were going to be applied in all the hypothetical cases in which we occupied the roles now occupied by others,'[6] so that in accepting capital punishment for murderers I am prepared to accept it for myself if I commit murder, and in rejecting capital punishment I am prepared to reject it for the person who murders me or a member of my family.

But there is one major loophole in the moral argument of those who support or accept capital punishment, which derives from the fact that any legal system, no matter how rigorous its procedures, is bound on occasion to err and to find some innocent person guilty. While it may cogently be argued that within a legal system there can be no enforceable right of an innocent person not to be found guilty and punished for an offence he has not committed,[7] capital punishment is qualitatively different from all other punishments in its finality and in permitting no possibility for the remedy or amelioration of a mistake as to guilt. While accepting the moral force of this argument, I do not feel it is of such an order as to establish the claim that the maintenance of capital punishment in law for any form of deliberate killing constitutes a gross violation of the right to life which all states have an immediate fundamental duty to protect.[8] Opinion is moving, however, in that direction, as witnessed in particular in the Sixth Protocol of the European Convention on Human Rights which provides for the abolition in peace time of capital punishment, subject to certain reservations. Capital punishment is, of course, morally unacceptable if it is applied discriminately as between persons of different race, colour, descent, national or ethnic origin or religion, or on grounds of sex.

More immediately pressing problems are raised in relation to contraception, abortion, euthanasia and suicide. The debate is between those who view these problems in terms of a fundamental moral duty to choose to live and to maintain life, requiring legal restriction or prohibition in these areas, and those who see them in terms of a fundamental right to choose whether or not to live or maintain life, which right of choice ought to be legally recognized and possibly facilitated. The fundamental difference in these two approaches is at its sharpest and simplest in relation to suicide. Traditional Christian morality teaches that life is a gift of God which it is each man's duty to maintain and respect both in himself and in others. Consequently suicide, euthanasia and abortion are equally wrong when deliberately undertaken.

The moral situation is different with regard to contraception, both because what is at issue is the prevention of the conception of life not its maintenance, and because the Catholic Church as the main upholder of traditional Christian teaching has in recent years come to accept 'safe-period' intercourse as a morally acceptable form of birth-control for married couples. In his Encyclical Letter *Humanae Vitae* Pope Paul VI justified the Church's distinction between safe-period intercourse and other forms of contraception, including 'the pill', on the ground that it is only in the former case that 'husband and wife are ready to abstain from intercourse during the fertile period as often as for reasonable motives the birth of another is not desirable.'[9] Elizabeth Anscombe, a lay Catholic and Professor of Philosophy at Cambridge, has argued that one must further distinguish in these two cases between the moral rightness of the thing that is being done and the intention with, and purpose for, which it is being done. Though she accepts that the intention and purpose of both acts is to avoid the conception of children she asserts that the use of contraceptives of any kind purposely renders the act of intercourse infertile, whereas safe-period intercourse is in itself a perfectly normal act of married intercourse.[10] It is difficult, however, to see why in terms of Christian or other morality rendering the act of intercourse infertile should be regarded as morally reprehensible in itself, where the purpose for which it is carried out is morally acceptable, i.e. to permit both married love and a planned family.

But even if one accepts, as many Catholics in their sexual practice do not accept, that Catholic morality as distinct from Catholic authority requires Catholics to abstain from the use of contraceptives, that provides no justification for a legal denial of contraceptive facilities to non-Catholics or Catholics. Yet it is precisely such a legal denial that the Church urges on the Governments of the world and that it uses its great influence to maintain in Catholic countries.[11] In a world almost collapsing under the burden of an ever more rapidly increasing population, there can be no moral case for legally preventing those who so wish from engaging in contraceptive practices which destroy no life, harm no person and neither degrade the marriage relationship nor undermine the family. Laws forbidding contraception constitute a fundamental violation of human rights.

The moral problem of abortion is much more complex. At one extreme stand the traditionalists for whom abortion is a moral degradation, acceptable only in those few cases where interference with the unborn child is an unintended, though foreseen, side-effect of procedures necessary to save the mother's life;[12] at the other the libertarians demanding the unqualified right of every woman to do what she wills with her own body. The latter position is not difficult to dispose of, since the child in the womb is not a 'woman's own body' in the sense in which her arm or leg is. To abort a six-month-old foetus is to kill a creature capable of being delivered alive by Caesarian section and is an act in no way morally different from killing a six-month-old premature-born baby. The strict traditionalist case is of stouter construction. It rests on the assertion that life begins with the act of conception and that there is no difference between the moral position of the human zygote and that of the new-born child, each having an equal right to live. In between we have the moderate liberal stance that there is a fundamental physical difference between the nature of the zygote and the fully-developed foetus, such that one can characterize the latter, but not the former, as 'human'. Even though it is not possible to say precisely when human characteristics *are* present one can say when they *are not*, and consequently can establish when abortion is legally permissible; that is when it does not involve the deliberate ending of a human life.

Roger Wertheimer has persuasively argued that either the traditional or the liberal moral position is tenable and that neither can be proven; since the ascription of humanity to some point in the embryo's development is not a matter of fact but of different moral conceptions.[13] If no genuine truth-value can be assigned to the assertion that the foetus is a human being, one cannot establish a human right to abortion in the strong sense of a right which it would be wrong for any society not to secure for its members by the provision of the requisite facilities. It would also imply that no violation of the right to life is entailed where a society makes abortion facilities available to pregnant women provided that it is not permitted after the time when the foetus might be safely delivered prematurely. Abortion would be unacceptable in human rights terms only where it involved the violation of the human rights of a human, living being, as distinct from a non-viable foetus. Subject to this important reservation, abortion on demand would not appear to constitute a clear violation of human rights. One would not therefore hold, for example, that the European Court of Human Rights had a duty under Article 2(1) of the European Convention, which provides that 'Everyone's right to life shall be protected by law', to strike down legislation from any Community state granting such a legal right.[14]

Even if this view is accepted one might still have grave moral reservations about a law permitting the abortion of any non-viable foetus. There are strong grounds for arguing that a positive moral justification is required for the destruction of a human embryo, embodying as it does from the moment of conception the potential for human existence: a potential, moreover, which will in the majority of cases be realized if it is not interfered with.[15] No moral grounds can be adduced for permitting abortion as a mere convenience of timing or as a normal method of birth control. In contrast there are strong moral grounds for legally permitting abortion in substantiated cases of rape, severe danger to the mother's life or health, or the risk of the birth of a severely handicapped child; not merely in the negative sense of not prosecuting doctors who carry out such abortions, but in the positive sense of according to such women a right of access to required medical facilities in communities where these can reasonably be made available.

One final point which is often overlooked is that the expectant mother is not the only person with a rights interest in the developing embryo; the father too has an interest which ought to be considered and provided for both in law and in practice. While the father could never substantiate a moral right to an abortion against the mother's wishes, or a right to prevent an abortion necessary to safeguard the mother's life or health, or the birth of a severely handicapped child, it ought to be possible for him to do so where the expectant mother, especially an unmarried or separated mother, wants the abortion for personal convenience.[16]

A discussion of abortion leads naturally on to the even more vexed and emotionally charged issue of the euthanasia of severely handicapped babies. What is at issue here is not whether parents have an inherent moral right to decide whether a child of theirs should live or die, since there can be no general parental right of infanticide, but whether there are any circumstances in which the interests of the child entitle loving parents to seek to end the life of a child so handicapped that it could never lead a normal independent life. It will help to understand the nature of the problem if it is looked at by reference to a particular birth abnormality, spina bifida.

Of every thousand conceptions between 20 per cent and 30 per cent will be spontaneously aborted; most of these natural abortions exhibit features of abnormality. A further 2 per cent will be stillborn and 4 per cent will be born with severe defects. Approximately 0.3 per cent of new born babies suffer from spina bifida, in a high proportion of cases to a moderate or severe degree. In severe cases the infant is born with a meningomyelocele, a protruding sac, not usually covered with skin, filled with cerebrospinal fluid and containing a defective spinal cord. As a result the infant is paralysed below the level of the lesion, and suffers loss of bladder and bowel control, and possibly mental retardation. Until recently no treatment was available and the great majority of spina bifida babies died naturally within the first year. 'Vigorous treatment', however, is now available which enables a significantly higher proportion to survive, but subject to varying degrees of grave disability. The treatment is prolonged, an average of two years in hospital in two-week spells during the first five years, and very expensive. One study of 323 'vigorously treated' children in Britain found 134 still alive after eight to twelve years – about half had shunts draining excess cerebrospinal fluid in the brain (many had an IQ below 80), 40 per cent were totally incontinent, 43 per cent had chronic urinary infections and only seventeen could walk unaided. Against this the minority of babies who receive no treatment and survive beyond their first year do so under conditions markedly worse than those of treated babies. Doctors are sharply divided over whether all spina bifida babies ought to be 'vigorously' treated and on whether it is morally wrong to withhold such treatment in some cases.[17]

The starting point of any discussion of this problem in human rights terms must be the right of the handicapped child to live and to be given treatment to overcome or reduce his handicap, and to have special facilities and education to assist him to live as full a life as possible. No moral doubts exist concerning the right to life of the deaf, dumb, blind or crippled child, 'natural survivors' who have always been with us. Doubts and difficulties arise only with the much more serious degrees of handicap to be found in conditions like spina bifida, which in the past resulted in the natural early death of the child. Recent advances in medical and surgical techniques, however, have changed this, leaving the parents of a spina bifida baby with the responsibility of bringing up a partly paralysed, incontinent, crippled, mentally-retarded child who may well survive them. Has society the moral right legally to impose such dreadful burdens on ordinary, unsuspecting parents?

The strict traditionalist view is that every effort must be made to save the life of every delivered child, no matter how deformed or how brief its life expectancy, even with treatment. But, coupled with the traditionalist claim that there is no moral difference between the foetus at any stage and the delivered child, this would lead to the moral conclusion that, just as the medical profession has a duty to do everything possible to keep defective children alive who would die if nature took her course, so it has an equal duty to seek to find ways of preventing nature's course in spontaneously securing the abortion of millions of deformed foetuses each year. The prospect of medical technology being used to ensure that in fifty or sixty years' time one in four or five of all births were of abnormal children has only to be considered to be rejected as a fearful distortion of any conception of a human right to life. On the contrary one would wish medical techniques and practices to be developed so that it would be possible in virtually all cases to diagnose deformity in an embryo at an early stage so that the foetus might, if the mother wished, be aborted, thus reducing to a minimum the number of deformed babies born.

If this view is accepted it follows that it cannot be a prime duty of the medical profession to devote themselves to ensuring the survival of an increasing number of increasingly deformed and suffering children, as distinct from saving the lives, alleviating the suffering and reducing the incapacities of children capable of living full or near-full lives. While the dividing line can never be sharp, and will change as medical techniques change, it is possible to identify those conditions, like spina bifida, where the medical authorities are agreed on the exceptional nature of the deformity and where even those opposed to treatment being withheld can understand the reasons which lead their colleagues as devoted members of the medical profession to support non-treatment. In this restricted area parents should have a legal right to refuse their consent to treatment (subject to appeal by the appropriate medical authorities to the courts) and doctors a right not to be prosecuted for withholding treatment. It is doubtful, however, whether the case for a legal right of parents to withhold consent and of doctors to withhold treatment is sufficiently strong to justify its incorporation as a universal human right which no state with the necessary resources has any right to deny, even when it conflicts with deep-rooted religious principles based on respect for human life. It should rather be seen as a legitimate claim for legal recognition involving no infringement of the human right to life.

But should one go further and argue, in the very restricted range of congenitally deformed children whose defects will mean a limited, distorted life, that doctors should, with parental consent, have the right not simply to withhold treatment (passive euthanasia) and let nature take its course, but to accelerate death (active euthanasia)? Dr John M. Freeman writes 'Having seen children with unoperated meningomyeloceles lie around the ward for weeks or months untreated, waiting to die, one cannot but feel that the highest form of medical ethic would have been to end the pain and suffering, rather than wish the patient would go away.' He concludes 'It is time that society and medicine stopped perpetuating the fiction that withholding treatment is ethically different from terminating life.'[18] If, as has been argued above, women have a basic right to secure the termination by abortion before birth of a foetus where there is a substantial risk of abnormality, does it not logically follow that they have a similar right to secure the termination after birth of the life of an infant with medically substantiated, non-correctable serious abnormalities?

While there is little biological difference between a foetus and an infant there is a vast difference in the way in which human beings view them. It is a new-born child, not the foetus, which inspires love and feelings of concern, precisely because it is the child, not the foetus, which requires love and devotion. Human rights derive not from man's abstract reason alone but from the whole man, as a thinking-feeling being. Consequently a distinction between the way the foetus and the new-born child is treated in rights is appropriate. Thus one may claim the right of a pregnant woman to secure an abortion where there is a risk of an abnormality, like blindness, which could never justify active or passive euthanasia after birth (i.e. if the blind child was born very prematurely and required treatment to keep it alive for the first few days or weeks). It is questionable whether Dr Freeman is speaking for the majority of laymen or doctors when he denies any ethical difference between withholding treatment and terminating life. Most people would probably, as Lord Cohen avers, be prepared to apply A.H. Clough's observation 'Thou shalt not kill, but need'st not strive officiously to keep alive.'[19] There is the feeling that active euthanasia for deformed newborn children is dangerous in that it more readily opens the way to embark on an active policy of classifying certain categories of persons as 'unfit' and then painlessly 'putting them down', as in Nazi Germany. For these reasons it seems unwise to claim a moral right of parents to have the life of a severely handicapped child terminated by medical intervention.

One major difficulty that we face in dealing with the morality of euthanasia for abnormal babies is that we are unable to take account of the wishes of the infant, since the infant can have no wishes. While parents and doctors may try to think themselves into the position of the child which the deformed infant will grow into, and conclude that they would, or would not, wish to survive in that condition rather than not-be, the status and worth of any such judgements is unclear. Nor is it particularly helpful to construct, as Professor Hare does, a dialogue between an abnormal new-born child, which if operated on will survive as severely handicapped but if not will die, and 'the next in the queue' child which the parents will produce, and on this basis seek to establish that there would be agreement between the two children on the superior claims of the latter to live, justifying leaving the child that is abnormal to die.[20]

The intractable problem here of determining the wishes of the person whose life is under review vanishes as soon as we are dealing with adult beings capable of rational choice, and of understanding the meaning and significance of death.[21] In human rights terms the right to take one's own life is perhaps the most natural of all rights of choice. Its basic requirement is simply that those who unsuccessfully attempt suicide should not be criminally punished for that attempt. A suffering patient should have the right to refuse any treatment necessary to prolong his life, but not to demand that others put him to death; although any society providing such 'exit' facilities under strictly controlled conditions should not thereby be held to be violating the right to life. No society, however, can have the right to terminate the life of any person without his consent; though it may be permissible, subject to stringent rules, to withhold life-support treatment from a patient who has been unconscious over a long period and who is medically judged incapable of regaining consciousness or of living as a sentient being.

While the central core of the right to life is the right not to be killed or threatened with killing, its moral perimeters are not restricted to that negative area. The right to life is seen in moral terms as the right not to be left to die or allowed to die, imposing on others reciprocal duties to provide assistance. In personal terms I have a moral right against you not to be left to die if you are in a position to prevent this, and you have an obligation so to act towards me: where the right and obligation will be the stricter the more urgent the help required and the less burdensome or dangerous its provision. There is clearly a qualitative difference between my cry for help as a *moral right*, while I lie seriously injured by the roadside, and my cry for help as a *moral plea*, while I am being beaten to death by a gang of thugs. The principle of reciprocity provides a rough moral guide in such situations. You should be ready to provide such assistance, at such personal inconvenience or risk as you think others ought to make available to you; but with the proviso that you are not entitled to opt out of all moral responsibility because of your readiness, assumed or real, to forfeit the assistance of others. My right not to be left to die is a fundamental moral right which you cannot deny on any count, other than that of danger to your own life. Though I may have forfeited my right to assistance, through having left another to die unaided, that does not absolve you from the duty of coming to my aid. But while the moral position of individuals is readily understood it is less apparent what it involves in terms of universal human rights principles to be incorporated in positive law. Although all societies recognize the reciprocal rights and duties of individuals standing in special relationships to one another (e.g. children and parents, patients and doctors) respectively to be sustained in life and to sustain life, the general obligation to sustain life has in modern societies been largely assumed by public authorities.[22] What were in simpler times, and are still in simpler societies, the moral rights and duties of individuals are now the legal rights of individuals and the legal duties of society.

All societies accept a general obligation to preserve and sustain the lives of their people in times of natural disaster – earthquake, hurricane, drought, flood, fire and above all, hunger and famine. With respect to the last of these, the Parties to the International Covenant on Economic, Social and Cultural Rights (ICES), in 'recognizing the fundamental right of everyone to be free from hunger,' have assumed responsibility to take 'individually and through international cooperation' the measures required 'to ensure an equitable distribution of world food supplies in relation to need,' (Article 11).[23]

The right to life as the right to freedom from hunger and famine may be broken down into two distinct parts: the rights of the hungry and starving against persons and authorities in their own country and their rights against those in other countries. The core of the right not to starve to death is a direct expression of the negative right not to be killed. No person or body may deliberately deprive any person of the food necessary for life, thereby causing his death or undermining his health and strength and lessening his chances of survival, whether by intention or as a necessary consequence of the action taken. Those subject to such conditions are entitled, either individually or collectively, to take steps to secure the food necessary to preserve themselves, provided that such steps are not at the expense of their fellow-sufferers and do not involve the risk of death or injury to innocent parties. The afflicted are also entitled to quit their own country and to be accepted as refugees in another country.[24]

The most serious and intractable problems arise where the body responsible for threatening and causing death is the state itself. In such circumstances there is the long-recognized natural right at last resort of sufferers, individually and collectively, to take such steps as are necessary to force the Government to relent. Non-sufferers in such a situation have a moral duty, even at some risk to themselves, to seek to mitigate the impact of the policies of death being pursued by the authorities. If all else fails those threatened with mass destruction, like the people of Cambodia being decimated by the Khmer Rouge, may appeal for outside intervention to overthrow the regime. Where the organs of the United Nations fail to take appropriate action under the United Nations Charter for the prevention and suppression of mass killings, as provided for in the Convention on the Prevention and Punishment of the Crime of Genocide,[25] individual states are entitled to intervene, provided that such intervention is directed to the purpose of prevention and suppression.

But have those many millions suffering the threat of death from hunger, rather than from the murderous policies of their own Governments, any valid claim to outside assistance? In attempting to deal with this question it is necessary to stress first the much more direct and incontestable claims existing against their own Government and people. The starving have a fundamental right to be fed, imposing on those in possession of or control over food a strict obligation to make it available. If the rich with abundance of food or of wealth translatable into food shut their eyes and close their doors, or if merchants hoard stocks or will only sell at grossly inflated prices so that death stalks the land, the starving have a natural right individually or in concert to take the food necessary for survival or to force food sales at just prices. The exercise of the natural right to ensure one's survival in this way will only arise, of course, if the public authorities are unable or unwilling to take action to make food available. If such authorities do not simply fail in their duty of acting to relieve starvation, but instead act against the starving in defence of the starvers, hoarders and profiteers, they forfeit all claim to obedience from the suffering.

The situation is less clear-cut where one is dealing not with crisis conditions of famine and starvation, calling for immediate action in special areas, but with permanent widespread conditions of hunger, leading not to the sight of dead bodies in the street but to premature death from ill-health and malnutrition. What rights does a hungry child in India have? While a particular child may have a rights claim to assistance valid against particular individuals based on special relationships, in the main the hungry do not have rights claims as individuals against individuals, but as members of the class of the hungry majority against the class of the rich well-fed minority and against their own Government. Since hunger is in many countries a permanent fact of stunted life for a majority of the population, with deep and multiple causes, it cannot be remedied, as the prospect of imminent death from starvation may be remedied as a last resort, by seizing from the rich-in-food the means for survival. The right of the hungry against the rich is not a natural right of seizure but a more limited fundamental right to exert moral pressure on the rich to carry out their moral duties to their fellow-poor. These non-enforceable moral duties are those of making personal contributions to the relief of suffering and of using their power and personal influence over the public authorities to secure effective action to alleviate hunger. The hungry, for their part, have a basic right to exert political pressure against the Government to require it to fulfil its fundamental obligations to ensure that all are fed.

In the light of these considerations one may approach the question of the rights of the starving and hungry of the poor states of the world against the inhabitants and Governments of the rich states. If we return to our starting point, where one individual on the verge of starving to death directly confronts another individual with sufficient to save the other's life without danger to his own, it is manifest that the former's natural moral right to assistance and the latter's natural moral duty to assist is not materially altered if the individuals come from different countries. The situation changes, however, when the confrontation takes place across the frontier with a famine state. For while the moral relationship is unaltered, it cannot be so confidently asserted that the person starving has a natural right to enforce his right to be fed by stealing food by stealth or by force, if assistance is refused by those across the border. If one turns to the unfortunately not uncommon situation where floods of starving refugees pour across a border, one cannot substantiate a claim for such groups to an overriding natural right to seize food from the indigeneous population; even if it were possible to ensure that the upshot was not the replacement of the former by the latter as the starving group. Men cannot claim a natural right to take action to secure for themselves the fundamental human rights they are entitled to have secured to them under the law, except where the political authorities responsible for their realization and protection blatantly fail or refuse to do so. It is impossible, therefore, to accept the assertion by men deprived of human rights in their own society of a claimed natural right forceably to secure those rights against the members of another society engaged in the lawful exercise of rights secured to them by their own Government. On the contrary the latter have a right to have their rights protected by their Government against the assaults of even starving invaders.

If starving refugees cannot establish enforceable natural rights against the inhabitants of the country they seek to flee to, have they any substantial moral claim against the government of that society? The answer would appear to be a qualified 'yes'. Starving men, women and children have a fundamental right not to be forced to starve along the frontier fence or to be rounded up and pushed back over the border; but that right cannot be claimed as an unconditional human right against the border state. Such a state is under a moral obligation to put the human rights needs of its own citizens before those of outsiders, just as parents are under an obligation to put the needs of their own children before those of others. A Government cannot be held to be under a strict obligation to take in and feed tens of thousands of starving refugees at the cost of causing severe hunger amidst its own population simply because it is the adjoining state; especially since such states are, in the geographical nature of things, likely themselves to be poor states with food and hunger problems of their own. What proximity imposes on Governments is a strict obligation, resting on all who find themselves faced with lives in danger which only they are in a position to save, to take all steps possible to prevent death, even at inconvenience or risk to themselves. In particular Governments, like individuals, must be prepared to initiate life-saving action even where they lack the capacity to sustain it unless others render support. It is on those others, and especially the rich states of the world, that the obligation falls individually and collectively to do what is necessary to enable the refugee-receiving nation to cope. The practical difficulty is that it is not possible to establish what share of the total responsibility for the relief of famine should be borne by each of the individual rich states. Consequently it is not possible for those states suffering from famine, or its effects through an influx of refugees, to make specific rights claims for assistance against particular rich states. Instead what we have are *appeals* for help from the suffering states and *gifts* of relief from the affluent determined at their own discretion.

The problem of saving the starving from death is part of a much larger problem of alleviating the hunger of untold millions who suffer ill-health, half-living and half-lives. The realization of 'the right of everyone to be free from hunger' is a much more complex and more difficult task than the provision of food relief to meet crisis situations. Yet it is at the very heart of giving meaning to the right to life. Whatever the agencies to be used and the methods to be followed, it requires that the nations of the world commit themselves to some programme for survival with each of the richer nations regularly making available a minimum proportion of their annual wealth to the poorer, and the latter accepting the need to cooperate with development agencies to ensure funds and resources are properly used.[26] The right of the poor and hungry to live is, by the nature of the varied causes of their wretched condition and the range of possible remedies for its alleviation, not a right which they themselves can directly enforce against the rich nations of the world. What the poor and their Governments have is a fundamental human right to the needed assistance which could be made available, a right which *ought* to be internationally enforceable against those nations. What is at issue here is not the use of sanctions to ensure that rich states fulfil externally imposed aid obligations, but the building up of sufficient moral and social pressure, from within and without, to ensure that these states themselves undertake and implement obligations sufficient to meet the needs of the poor states. But most important of all the satisfaction of needs has to be conceived, not in terms of meeting food deficits (as in a refugee camp), but in co-operating with producers to increase food production in ways compatible with the realities of rural life, having prime regard to the special requirements of the very poor in the community concerned.

Down the ages the two great harbingers of death have been famine and war. If the right to life is the right not to die of hunger, must it not equally be a right not to be killed in war? But although the moral issue appears the same, the moral context is different. Hunger is a condition normally arising through natural causes of neglect and is only rarely deliberately inflicted as an end in itself or to secure other ends. Hunger has always been seen as an evil which ought always to be alleviated, imposing moral obligations on those in a position to do so. War, on the other hand, was presented in traditional morality as an instrument which, though evil in its form, might be justified in terms of the ends it served. In particular it was, and is still, accepted that states are morally entitled to defend themselves against outside attack. Indeed one may go further and say that it is in the nature and purpose of political societies that they assume an obligation to protect the community, and that to this end they have a right to require members of the community to take up arms and risk their lives in its defence. In a world of independent nation states it is not possible to claim an unqualified moral right of citizens not to have to risk their lives in war.[27] But it does not follow that every society can claim an unqualified right to require its citizens to risk their lives in any war it becomes engaged in. Whether such a claim can validly be made will depend on the nature of the war concerned, both with regard to its purpose and the manner in which it is waged – principles which received strong endorsement at the Nuremberg trials of the Nazi war leaders. A man has a moral right not to fight in, or to support, a war which he holds to be unjust. It is difficult, however, to see how such a right could be legally accorded in any political system, still less required of all systems.[28] If a man holds his own country to be engaged in an unjust war he has a moral right to evade participation, not a human right to be legally exempted from participating.

With regard to the methods of waging war there is a well-established tradition of rules or laws of war laying down principles of conduct to which states are expected to adhere, embodied in international agreements to which states are parties. Prohibitions under such agreements, and under the general principles of international law, are held to be binding not only upon states but upon individuals, especially members of the armed forces. It is left to the individual state parties to rectify breaches of the rules of war through domestic action, no provision being made for international supervision or enforcement. It can, however, be argued that under Article 6 of ICPR (which is not subject to derogation in time of public emergency, such as war), states and individuals have an express obligation not to infringe the requirement that 'no one shall be arbitrarily deprived of life', a requirement which would cover the deliberate killing of prisoners or civilians. In order to make clear that the requirements of the rules of war are binding against any plea of 'obedience to superior orders' a number of Western states, including the United Kingdom, have incorporated in their military regulations a section expressly prohibiting soldiers from committing war crimes or crimes against humanity under any circumstances.[29]

A different situation arises where the objection raised is not to the justness of a particular war, but to the immorality of war itself. Those who have a deep conscientious objection to the taking of human life for whatever reason hold a position which is morally unassailable and personally enforceable; since there is no way in which a person can be made to fight and kill. What is at issue here is whether such persons have a fundamental right not to be punished for refusing to fight, having regard to the fact that it is perfectly possible to devise machinery for granting conscientious exemption from military service. In terms of the right to life conscientious objectors would have a minimum right not to be subject to military conscription involving a liability to execution for refusing to obey orders to kill other human beings. There is no objection in principle, however, to such persons being required to perform non-combatant services which may in themselves be dangerous, particularly services concerned with the saving of lives.[30] What cannot be doubted, however, is that any right of freedom of belief and expression will cover the right of those of pacifist persuasion to hold their views and to express them publicly. States which proclaim their dedication to peace and their opposition to the perpetual threat of Armageddon have no grounds in reason or in conscience for stifling those who claim that wars will only end when men and women refuse to fight them.

But, while the right not to be required *to kill* in war is of crucial importance for a limited number of individuals, the crucial issue for the world at large is whether it is possible to establish in any meaningful form a general right not *to be killed* in war. The realist answer has always been that given a world divided between scores of independent states with conflicting interests, aims and ideologies, war is a natural and inevitable ingredient in international relations. What might be secured was the limitation of warfare, and therefore of killing, as far as practicable, to direct combatants. It is on these terms that there was derived from ancient and medieval custom and practice the modern rules of war embodied in the Geneva and other Conventions, respecting the rights of non-combatants and prisoners of war.[31] Modern warfare has made the distinction between combatants and non-combatants increasingly difficult to maintain, having regard to the crucial combative role played by civilians in producing the means of war and of the methods, especially aerial methods, used to destroy enemy war capacity. These tensions came to a grotesque and terrible head in the nuclear obliteration of Hiroshima and Nagasaki, six weeks *after* the signing in San Francisco of the Charter of the United Nations affirming the signatories' resolve to 'save succeeding generations from the scourge of war'.[32]

The awesome threat posed by nuclear weapons has led to attempts by the nuclear-armed powers (in particular the USA and USSR) to reach agreement on nuclear disarmament and by the non-aligned states to secure a ban on the use of nuclear weapons. The latter initiative resulted in the 1961 United Nations General Assembly Declaration on the Prohibition of the Use of Nuclear and Thermo-Nuclear Weapons insisting that 'Any State using nuclear and thermo-nuclear weapons is to be considered as violating the Charter of the United Nations, as acting contrary to the laws of humanity and as committing a crime against mankind and civilization.'[33] The United States and other Western Powers voted against the Declaration.[34] They also refused to renounce the right to use nuclear weapons in response to a conventional military attack on the grounds that to do so would be to encourage an attack by the much stronger Soviet conventional forces. Instead they have developed a whole range of tactical 'theatre' nuclear weapons designed to deal with any Soviet military invasion of Western Europe without having to have direct resort to strategic nuclear weapons.

That nuclear war on even a relatively limited scale would be horrendous for those affected, and on a major scale calamitous for all mankind, is neither capable of being, nor is, denied. There is no realistically conceivable situation which could justify either the first use of nuclear weapons or their use in response to a nuclear attack, since there is no remotely acceptable moral end which either use could serve. As Jonathan Glover persuasively argues – 'when we think soberly about the worst hypothetical choice in the world, it is hard not to conclude that a Nazi society, including the extermination camps, would be less terrible than a major nuclear war.'[35] But it does not directly follow that to threaten to use nuclear weapons against an aggressor for the purpose of deterring aggression is morally unwarranted. The dilemma which arises, however, is that for the threat to have deterrent effect it has to be credible and it is extremely difficult, though perhaps not impossible, to see how such credibility could be maintained over time, if it were not based on a genuine commitment to carry it out in the circumstances specified. There is no reason to doubt the resolve of the presently armed nuclear powers to carry out their threats.

In seeking to make some sense of this complex and frightening lunatic situation we may resort to two simple truths. The first is that if war breaks out between the United States and Russia it will mean the end of the world as we know it, leaving a hell where, as President Kennedy foresaw, the living will envy the dead. The second is that as the nuclear powers continue to build up ever more accurate, speedy and lethal weapons, the likelihood of such a calamity occurring by malfunction, accident or local command error within our own lifetime or that of our children grows closer to near-certainty. There are many who argue from this that the only way to avoid ultimate catastrophe is through unilateral nuclear disarmament, and that all the nuclear-armed powers have an unqualified obligation to mankind to act accordingly. But since all such powers, and especially the USA and USSR, are resolutely opposed to unilateralism, such a fundamental shift of policy could only be expected if new leaders and new policies could be forced upon the respective nations through a great concerted and irresistible build-up of resolute, organized public opinion. Under present conditions it is only in Western states that such a build-up would be permitted to surface, let alone become a major political force directed against the states' defence policies and political leaders. To demand nuclear unilateral disarmament to remove the threat of nuclear war is, in effect, to demand unilateral United States nuclear disarmament. Unilateral British action might at best help to strengthen the unilateral movement in the United States and encourage United States readiness to take nuclear disarmament initiatives: at worst it might lead to a United States withdrawal from Europe and a retreat into nuclear isolationism.

The right to life unquestionably assumes its most urgent and universal form as the right not to be subjected to the horrors of modern warfare, and above all of nuclear warfare. The right is one which may be secured only through international action and international agreement, agreement which cannot be realized except through influence being brought to bear *from within* on the governments of the respective national states. The principles which need to be followed are not in dispute, the difficulties lie in securing their implementation under conditions of suspicion, fear and prejudice, bred by and feeding on conflicting ideologies, values and goals.

The moral principles which states ought urgently to follow may be simply stated:

(i) moral duty of all governments to 'refrain in their international relations from the threat or use of force against the territorial integrity or political independence of any state' (Article 2, Charter of the United Nations);

(ii) moral duty of all governments to seek agreement on disarmament, especially nuclear disarmament, with a view to substantially reducing the level of, and expenditure on, weapons of war;

(iii) moral duty of all men to seek to persuade the governments of their respective states to fulfil their obligations under (i) and (ii) above.

From these principles we may derive a fundamental right – the right of men and women in all states to work and campaign for peace – a right directed in the first instance against their own Governments.

3
The Right to Liberty

Moral rights cannot exist where there is no conception of individual liberty. It is not the recognition of the distinctive nature of rational choice as such, but the high value placed on each individual person exercising that capacity in his or her own way that permits the emergence of a political tradition grounded on moral rights. The concept of liberty thus lies at the heart of the doctrine of fundamental human rights. But, though this truth is universally recognized the nature of theaconcept of liberty itself remains a matter of continuing debate. This absence of agreement is less inhibiting than at first appears, since while a general right of liberty cannot be formulated except on the basis of some specific conception of what liberty is or ought to be seen to be, particular liberty rights do not have to be derived from a claimed general right to liberty. Indeed, there are good reasons for resisting the temptation to assert a general right to liberty, both because of the inherently contestable nature of the underlying conception of liberty which it will express, and because of the questionable capacity of such a claimed general right to support a structure of specific fundamental liberty rights as rights of each against all.[1]

It is instructive, however, to look briefly at one celebrated version of a general right to liberty, that put forward by Professor H.L.A. Hart in 'Are There Any Natural Rights?' Professor Hart's thesis is that, given the recognition of the moral value of individual freedom, each and every man and woman capable of choice has a natural right to be free. He or she

(i) 'has the right to forbearance on the part of all others from the use of coercion or restraint against him save to hinder restraint or coercion', and

(ii) 'is at liberty to do (i.e. is under no obligation to abstain from) any action which is not one coercing or restraining or designed to injure other persons.'[2]

Hart claims that, in the absence of special rights arising out of special transactions or relationships between individuals, all men and women have a general right to forbearance under the terms of (i) above. But this claim cannot be sustained since it takes no account of the necessary and legitimate role of the Government in organized society. The state is entitled through its appointed officers to interfere with the lives and activities of its citizens by imposing taxes or enacting laws (e.g. planning laws) which have purposes other than hindering coercion or restraint. It is only in a state of nature where men live socially together, but without a framework of law, that men can be said to have a natural right to be free along the lines Hart lays down. While Hart's general right to liberty cannot, therefore, function as a fundamental human right his distinction between the two forms or aspects of the right to liberty, as a right to non-coercion and the right to non-interference, is valuable for analysing and distinguishing particular fundamental liberty rights, established as those rights of which no man or woman may be deprived or denied by any person or body.

Before turning to consider particular substantive rights it is important to draw attention to one fundamental constitutive liberty right. Given the nature of the concept of law as the embodiment of sanction-backed rules of society and of human rights as fundamental entitlements which the law ought everywhere to uphold and protect, one can deduce the following right: 'all persons have a fundamental liberty right not to be subject to coercion, restraint or punishment by the state authorities for doing any act which is either specifically permitted by law, or not specifically prohibited by law.'[3] This constitutive liberty right exists quite independently of the status of the action concerned in substantive human rights terms.

Liberty rights comprise a large and complex area of human rights and this chapter is restricted to a consideration of those rights of non-coercion and non-interference inherent in or closely associated with that most unfree of all human conditions, that of slavery, viz:

    freedom from slavery
    freedom from forced labour
    freedom of movement and residence
    freedom of marriage

Subsequent chapters will deal with freedom of belief and expression (Ch. 4) and freedom of association and assembly (Ch. 5).

Freedom from slavery

The great classical scholar William L. Westermann characterized the 'hard core' of slavery as embedded in the concept of 'the right of complete ownership of one human being by another, with control by the master of the physical powers and the mobility of the slave. Ideologically the slave has no individuality, no legal personality apart from that of his owner. Customarily, in the eyes of the law the slave has no male parent.'[4] The classical Greek's own conception of slavery is made clear in the Delphic inscriptions recording slave manumissions, which list the newly acquired liberties of the freed slave – to be his own master in law, not to be subject to seizure as property, to have freedom of action and freedom of movement.[5]

For the Greeks slavery was an established universal feature of the social and economic life of the time and as such accepted by masters and slaves, philosophers and ordinary men. It might be justified on three grounds. Firstly it was universally accepted in the ancient world that the victorious power in war had an absolute right over the persons of the vanquished.[6] Since, except for those captives able to ransom themselves, the only conceivable alternative to slavery was death, slavery might appear as the preferred choice or even the right of the captive. In these terms captive slavery may be morally justified as an outcome which I am prepared to accept for myself on the same terms as I would claim it against others. Secondly the great majority of slaves, both captive and purchased, were not Greeks but foreigners; and foreigners were regarded by Greeks as barbarians, abject subjects of despotic rulers fitted by nature to be slaves, in contrast with their own position as free citizens of free states.[7] Thirdly, as seen by Aristotle, the natural slave was one who was more than a beast but less than a man, sharing in reason but lacking the capacity to make moral choices for himself. The natural slave was thus not fitted to live a free life and required a master. The slave–master relationship was mutually beneficial – the good slave served his master faithfully and the good master looked after and cared for the wants of the slave. The natural slave might therefore be expected to have sufficient reason to recognize his need for a master, and to recognize that the slave–master relationship was right for them both.

Theories of natural slavery were open to criticism on many scores.

Firstly, natural slavery could not be used to justify the existing institution of slavery, since that involved both the enslavement of former free men who had shown themselves capable of moral choice and the use of slaves in positions of moral responsibility as tutors, nurses or, in Rome, as physicians. Secondly, there was a fundamental contradiction between the notion of a natural slave and the reality of forced enslavement. Since the natural slave, unlike an animal, participated in rationality to the degree that he could apprehend the reason for his condition, natural slavery should have been based on consent not force. Thirdly, justice in natural slavery would require not only that unnatural slaves be released but that natural slaves among the free be enslaved, which was completely unacceptable to all free men. Fourthly, a conception like that of the natural slave, grounded on assertions of fundamental differences in reasoning capacity, required a specification of what those differences were and how they might be objectively recognized and tested. In the absence of such established criteria the theory of natural slavery acted as an ideological support of slavery as established, instead of a determination of what constituted justice in slavery.

But in a very real sense all these criticisms are peripheral, in that while they point to weaknesses in the theory of natural slavery or to difficulties in its application, they do not destroy the premise that some men are slaves by nature. The weakness of that premise is shown up as soon as we ask the question 'What are slaves for?' Slaves existed to work, thus relieving freemen of that burden and enabling them to devote themselves to more enjoyable or higher pursuits. But the fact that a slave worked, even if under supervision and only at a menial occupation, is indicative of a level of reasoning and earning capacity consistent with living in freedom. The fundamental flaw in the natural slave thesis, however, is not logical but moral. The fact that some persons may be incapable of living independent lives of their own does not justify their being enslaved and being used as tools to serve others' purposes. Such persons, like orphaned children, may require to be made subject to the authority of others, but under protective conditions designed to ensure that those others do not misuse that authority to promote their own selfish interests at the expense of the welfare and needs of those in their charge. Such a conception is quite at variance with slavery, which is based on the interests and rights of the master not of the slave.

The conception of man as a being capable of living a life of his own choosing, and of the freely chosen life as the life of highest value, requires the recognition that no man whether in nature or society has the right to enslave another. But should a man not have a right in freedom to choose to enslave himself to another? This apparent paradox of freedom is less difficult to resolve than at first appears. Firstly one may readily distinguish between a free choice and a forced choice. If my victorious assailant in battle offers me the alternative of death or slavery I may in all good conscience and sense accept slavery as the lesser evil. But there is nothing necessary or inevitable about this pair of choices: the alternative to death could be temporary service or temporary prisoner-of-war status. A strictly voluntary assumption of slavery as the most preferred choice is likely to be not only a very rare occurrence, but an indefensible one. Service or submission to the will of another does not require an assumption of servile status; indeed since slavery service operates under the ever-present threat of enforcement it is incompatible with free service or free submission. Voluntary enslavement makes no provision for a change of heart or will either by the slave who comes to regret his original free choice of unfreedom, or by the master who, tiring of his would-be lackey, casts him to one side or sells him to another.

Although no states in the world today openly uphold the institution of slavery, chattel slavery, including harem slavery, is still to be found in a number of countries. Slavery is most difficult to dislodge where the state's rulers are themselves the slave owners. Thus in Mauritania the Anti-Slavery Society of Britain estimates that out of a population of 1,500,000 there are 100,000 slaves owned overwhelmingly by members of the élite group of white Moors who dominate the government, the civil service, the judiciary and the police: the very people responsible for giving effect to the decree of 5 July 1980 abolishing the slavery which the independence constitution of 1960 had outlawed. The Mauritanian authorities' lack of devotion to the cause of slave abolition is still more strikingly evidenced by its harassment of the slave emancipation group, El Hor, and the imprisonment and torture of its leaders.[8] In liberty rights terms there is no more urgent and fundamental a need than action to remove the scourge and degradation of slavery. A much greater priority needs to be given by the United Nations to the removal of slavery than at present. A United Nations Anti-slavery inspectorate should be set up to monitor and report to the United Nations Working Group of Experts on Slavery in Geneva, and United Nations agencies and associated bodies should be urged to make the granting of economic and social aid dependent on effective action to eliminate slavery.

Freedom from forced labour

Forced labour is an integral feature of many forms of labour relationships other than that of chattel slavery. One way in which one may classify different forms of forced labour is by reference to how persons enter into the condition of bondage and to the permanency of that bond:

(i) *forced* into a *permanent* condition where one is required to perform work services which one is forbidden to quit.

This was the position in Russia of the free 'black' peasants made into serfs in the sixteenth and seventeenth centuries, of fugitive serfs assigned to state or private factories in the eighteenth, and of peasants forced into collective farms in the 1930s. The condition of permanent attachment to work-services may be made subject to restrictions or interferences making it analogous to slavery.

(ii) *born* into a *permanent* condition where one is required to perform work-services which one is forbidden to quit.

This was the position of Russian serfs until the emancipation of 1861 and of the Indian *colonos* of Bolivia until 1952. The *colonos* families were subject to a wide range of impositions; in addition to the basic corvée duty of three days a week with three persons, or four days with two, they were supervised by foremen with the right to mete out physical punishment and to impose fines for unsatisfactory work.

(iii) *voluntary entry* into a *permanent* condition where one is required to perform work-service which one is forbidden to quit.

Marc Bloch refers to numerous deeds of voluntary submission to serfdom in France around the ninth century.[9] One needs to distinguish, however, between voluntary entry as a free choice between available alternatives and as a forced choice between submission or ruin and starvation.

(iv) *voluntary entry* into a *temporary* condition where one is required to perform work-services which one is forbidden to quit; but where the condition, though temporary, commonly becomes or is designed to become *permanent*.

This usually takes the form of debt bondage and may arise either directly or indirectly. Thus the twelfth century *zakupy* indentured labourers of Kiev and the sixteenth century Russian *kabala* peasants freely entered into agreements which provided for their being granted loans to be repaid by working full-time for the creditor on terms which made it virtually impossible to pay back the capital borrowed. The nature of the servitude embodied in *kabala* debt bondage found recognition in those subject to this condition becoming known as *kabala* slaves.[10] In contrast the sugar plantations of the Chiama Valley in Peru were worked after 1895 by highland Indians recruited on short-period contracts which provided for an advance on wages paid in gold, but with wages paid in company tokens valid only in company bars and stores. Under these conditions free contract was itself the road to serfdom. The workers became enslaved to their debts and obliged to remain for life working on the plantations.[11] Debt bondage is distinguished from other conditions of servitude in that usually it does not legally bind the child 'while still in its mother's womb,' though in cases where the family was the borrower under a *kabala* contract the loan remained a charge against all members of the family for the rest of their lives.

The coercive element in permanent bondage has two aspects – the coercion involved in the act of embondment and the coercive nature of the bondage relationship itself. Physical incorporation into bondage against one's will constitutes a particularly flagrant invasion of one's right not to be forced to labour for others; but is, as we have seen, characteristic of only some forms of bondage and then primarily in the initial stages. But it is the grossness of the infringements imposed on the right to choose for oneself how one will live, inherent in permanent bondage, that constitutes the crux of the case against serfdom, rather than how that bondage is established. Consequently, while it is important to bring out the personal or social factors which effectively turn free-choice acceptance into forced-choice submission, it is permanent bondage itself which stands condemned. Those in enbondment are not necessarily without rights, but the rights they have are those accorded by the bondage system and designed to serve the interests of that system. Moreover, under conditions of permanent bondage it is difficult for a bondsman to establish such legal rights as he has against his master, since the latter is well placed to physically prevent access to the courts or to control their operation. Permanent bondage is akin to slavery in that it denies men and women freedom of movement and action, treating them not as human beings but as degraded, inferior creatures. Under The United Nations' Supplementary Convention on the Abolition of Slavery, the Slave Trade, and Institutions and Practices Similar to Slavery, 1956, member states are required to bring about the abolition of such institutions and practices.[12]

Debt bondage is a global phenomenon, to be found extensively, for example, in South America, the Middle East and the Indian Sub-continent. In India alone estimates of bonded labourers range from three to five million. Unlike slavery, but like child labour, debt bondage is often so bound-up with predominant economic practices built into the established social order that it is difficult to see how it can be significantly reduced without drastic and radical changes in the patterns of power and privilege within the societies concerned, changes which, even given resolute Government action, could only be brought into effect progressively over time. What can be immediately required is legislative action against practices designed to inveigle vulnerable members of the community into debt in order to subordinate them to a serf-like condition.

In most modern states forced labour in the strict sense exists in one of two main forms, both imposed by the state for limited periods – the labour of conscripts and the labour of prisoners. It has already been argued in Chapter 2 that, since every state has the duty to protect itself from military attack, it cannot reasonably be held to be a violation of the right to life to require citizens to risk their lives in their country's defence, or in pursuit of its legitimate interests in a just war. Many states in the world, including most states of Europe except the United Kingdom, however, now resort to compulsory peacetime military conscription, either universal or selective, to train the forces they require for their protection. Military conscription involves grave restrictions on freedom of movement, residence and work; but given the present state of international relations it is difficult to see how one could assert that it would constitute a violation of human rights on the part of any one state not to abolish military conscription even though enemies refused to do so.

In a major war it may be held necessary for the warring states to conscript a large part of the civilian labour force. The conscription of civilian labour in peacetime, on the other hand, may also be justified as a last resort in the event of and for the period of, a national emergency. What cannot be justified is the conscription of labour to deal with emergencies of the Government's own creation. Where conscription is introduced to deal with an emergency it needs to be under the labour conditions one associates with free labour rather than prison labour. A terrible example of gross Government incompetence in creating an emergency which it then sought to resolve by forced labour under inhuman conditions occurred in Ethiopia in 1980. After the expulsion of large farmers and the designation of the sesame-producing areas in the Humera region as a 'state farm', output fell dramatically. The Government responded by forcibly recruiting 45,000 persons from the towns who were herded together in camps under armed guards – those attempting to escape were shot. The conscripts were set to work under dreadful conditions without proper food, water or medical treatment. According to Ethiopian Government inspectors, 1626 died during the operation.[13]

The labour service required of legally convicted and sentenced prisoners is, like military service, expressly excluded from the categories of forced labour prohibited by the Forced Labour Convention of 1930 (Article 2.2).[14] That convention did, however, lay down a number of conditions designed to protect such prisoner-workers. In 1953 the International Labour Office (ILO) recognized that corrective labour camps (*gulags*) existed in all countries of the Soviet bloc as an integral part of the planned economy of those countries. More crucially the ILO established that persons were commonly assigned to such camps without prior trial and were there subject to harsh and often terrible conditions in contravention of the 1930 Convention to which these states were parties. The report led to the incorporation in the Abolition of Forced Labour Convention of 1957 of an article prohibiting forced labour 'as a means of political coercion or education, or as a punishment for holding or expressing political views or views ideologically opposed to the established political or economic system'.[15]

There is no objection in principle to convicted prisoners being required to work as part of their punishment; the objection is to the maintenance of a huge labour camp system permanently built into the economy and exploiting labour on such an exorbitant and reckless scale as to provide a constant demand on the security services to maintain a continuous supply of replacement prisoners. The economic viability of Soviet forced labour depends on the exaction of long hours of work under harsh conditions in contravention of the Forced Labour Conventions of 1930 and 1957 to which the USSR is party. The enforcement of these conventions would undermine that viability, thus undermining the labour camp system itself.

The inherent weakness of the Forced Labour Conventions in relation to prisoner-labour is that they rely for enforcement on the agency of the state involved, where that state is also the gaoler. While there is much to be said for the International Labour Office being given powers of inspection of prison labour, there is little or no prospect of this being acceptable to the Communist states. One is bound to conclude that the most elementary rights of prisoners will be secured only if the basic rights of freedom of expression and association can be sufficiently secured to permit the emergence of an effective public opinion.

Freedom of movement and residence
The right to move freely and to reside and work where one wills is one of the defining characteristics of a freeman as contrasted with a slave or an enbonded man. In a world of nation states this right has two dimensions – internal within the state concerned, and external outside that state. In its most restrictive form internal limitation involves persons being required to reside in a particular spot and not to leave it without express permission and may never be imposed by a private individual or private group except to detain a dangerous person until such time as the properly constituted authorities arrive. Only the state acting directly and openly can claim a legitimate right of detention. The state also has a strict obligation to apprehend and punish any persons who for any reason other than self-protection seek to detain others against their will. Thus, to take an all-too-familiar and striking example, state authorities are required to take such action as is necessary to secure the release of the hostages of a hijacked plane, irrespective of any sympathy for the cause the hijackers espouse.

But what of detention or enforced residence imposed by the state itself? Prison detention under humanitarian conditions imposed through due process of law on persons lawfully convicted of breaches of the criminal law, where that law is not itself in breach of fundamental human rights, raises no problems. More difficult issues, both theoretical and practical, are raised by the detention of persons in mental institutions and still more by their subjection to treatment without consent. Leaving aside the patently gross violation of human rights involved in the psychiatric detention of political dissidents in countries like the Soviet Union, the very conception of forcible detention of persons against their will for their own good is a disturbing one. Nevertheless it has to be accepted both that some persons are incapable of looking after themselves and that there are limits to the resources which can be made available to assist mentally handicapped persons. In human rights terms what can be demanded is that no person shall be confined in a mental institution except under stringent conditions designed to protect the rights of all those patently incapable of living their own lives in the community of their choice. That some persons find the presence of mentally handicapped persons distasteful or disturbing constitutes neither adequate nor relevant grounds for their compulsory detention. It might be claimed, however, that this position is morally warrantable provided that those who find the presence of mentally handicapped persons distasteful or disturbing genuinely accept that were they in that same condition they too ought to be put away 'for their own good'. Two responses to such an assertion may be made. The first is that the assertion has no value or meaning unless the person making it is aware of what 'that condition' actually consists, in its totality and not simply in particular expressions. The second and more fundamental is that in terms of individual liberty there can be no justification for depriving any unconvicted person of liberty through forcible incarceration unless he or she can be shown either to constitute a clear and present threat or danger to other members of the community or to his or her own self, or to be incapable of living alone even with some assistance.

Where compulsory commitment of a person to a mental institution is provided for it must be under regulations designed to protect the interests of the person committed. In particular the mentally disturbed need protection against the danger of errors or differences of professional judgement, to be provided with facilities for remedial treatment and to have their detention periodically renewed by an independent body charged with ensuring that only the dangerous or incapable are detained against their will. No one of us outsiders would agree now to our possible future commitment except under stringent conditions of this character. Nothing more terrible can be envisaged than to find oneself, whilst suffering from mental stress or breakdown, being locked up as a dangerously deranged person amongst seriously deranged persons, where the only alternative prospect to that prolonged agony is of gradually slipping into the very condition of derangement held to justify incarceration. The only acceptable principle in this area is a strong presumption on the part of all those armed with powers of commitment or retention in mental institutions that their overriding obligation is to seek for possible reasons for releasing not retaining their charges.

Mental detainees are in special need of protection against being subjected to treatment designed to eliminate or reduce disturbing behaviour at the expense of their will and consciousness. The aims, purposes and effects of treatment need to be subject to regular outside professional review and to public discussion. Mental institutions must not be sealed off from the outside world and there needs to be ready access for associations, like MIND in Great Britain, set up to protect the special interests and concerns of mental patients.

The detention of vagrants also raises basic questions regarding the right of individuals to liberty and security of the person. In the 'Vagrancy Cases' in 1971 the European Commission of Human Rights held that no violation of the right to liberty and security of the person had taken place since the complainants were dealt with as vagrants in accordance with the procedure prescribed by Belgian Law. The European Court of Human Rights held that there had been no violation because the definition of vagrants in Belgian Law did not appear to be in any way irreconcilable with the usual meaning of the term 'vagrant'.[16] In Belgian Law vagrants are defined as 'persons who have no fixed abode, no means of subsistence and no regular trade or profession', and a person found by a magistrate to be a vagrant will be detained either for between two and seven years, or for a period up to one year, according to the form of vagrancy.[17] While one may recognize that vagrancy laws may be applied paternalistically, in that they provide legal grounds for police authorities making accommodation and food available to 'down and outs', that is no reason for giving magistrates power to commit persons to compulsory detention for substantial periods. The detention of vagrants is usually justified on one of two grounds, that vagrants constitute a nuisance through their begging, drunkenness etc., or that they are idle good-for-nothings who deliberately live off society. On the first count if begging or drunkenness is held to be behaviour which should be legally proscribed it should be forbidden and punished as such, not treated as characteristic of vagrancy, meriting much longer periods of detention than would be acceptable as a punishment for drunkenness or begging.[18] On the second the number of those who deliberately choose to 'live off' society is considerably wider than the category of vagrants and will include those who deliberately avoid work or who do not do the work for which they are paid. In neither of the latter instances would compulsory detention be considered justified or appropriate in a free society. There seems, in particular, no case for subjecting to the threat of detention those who choose to live the life of the tramp or 'drop-out', as long as they do not break the law in so doing.

Quite different considerations are raised by the infliction of preventive detention, residence confinement or exile on convicted criminals. Though not in themselves inherently invalid forms of punishment, they are highly suspect in that they are often associated with arbitrary and oppressive rule. Where such measures are applied to whole groups of people, especially those of a particular religion, race, colour, national origin or ethnic group they constitute a flagrant violation of the right to non-discrimination. Even if the extreme exigencies of war may justify deporting persons of the same national origin or ethnic group as one's enemy from the border area, they will never justify doing so under such conditions or to such locations as to lead inevitably to large-scale suffering or death. Such dreadful suffering and torment accompanied the deportation of some million and a third persons from the southern part of Soviet Russia to the inhospitable lands of Siberia, Kazakstan, Central Asia and the Russian North between 1941 and 1944. The reason for the deportations was Stalin's fear that these people, including the Volga Germans (380,000), Chechens (400,000) and Crimean Tartars (200,000), would assist the invading German Army: fears which were understandable precisely because of these peoples' experience of the brutalities and iniquities of Soviet rule.

At an opposite pole to deportation is the requirement that designated persons are not permitted to leave their existing area of residence or place of work, either at all or only with the permission of the authorities. In so far as such restrictions are invariably applied discriminatorily, they are unwarranted on that count alone; whether one is dealing with collective farmers in Russia, tin-miners in Bolivia, or blacks on the reserves in South Africa. In each of these cases the persons concerned were prohibited or prevented from doing what they had a clear right to do, with a view to furthering the unwarranted interests of others or to overcoming difficulties resulting from doubtful or iniquitous policies pursued by the state authorities themselves. Those subject to such restrictions have a fundamental right to ignore the prohibitions and to quit, using such force as may be necessary against those who seek to contain them. Other members of society have an equally strong entitlement to help them in this endeavour. Restrictions on freedom of movement of this character can be justified only as a last resort in a strictly defined emergency situation, and under conditions which make it possible to question both the nature and duration of the emergency and the form of the restrictions concerned.

The situation is less clear-cut where one is dealing with the prevention or legal prohibition of residence or movement in specified parts of a country, since there may be valid grounds for excluding persons from entry into particular areas for a variety of reasons, e.g. to protect the environment or for defence and security purposes. Two points may perhaps be made. Firstly where residence or visiting is prohibited or restricted it should be applied without discrimination and be publicly made known and justified. Secondly ordinary members of society should not be forbidden to, or require permission to, visit areas of the country where other people ordinarily live, except in periods and conditions of proclaimed emergency. The basic right of citizens to freedom of movement and residence in their own country must necessarily be a right open to all in respect of the overwhelming mass of a state's land area, not a privilege to be granted at the discretion of the state bureaucracy.

The right not to be forced or legally required to leave one's own country is intrinsic to the concept of citizenship and it is difficult to see how its denial can ever be justified. Those who breach a country's laws should be punished according to the law, not forced into exile. But forced exile in the strict sense of thrusting a person at gun point over the border is a rare occurrence and one which, if practised on any scale, would raise serious problems of relations with the bordering state. More often one is dealing with the 'forced choice' acceptance of exile as an alternative to punishment or to continued harassment by the political authorities. In many cases offers of 'forced-choice' exile are made to those in the forefront of campaigns to secure the human rights which they are supposed to have already. But the most fearful and far-reaching examples of compulsory exile arise from agreements between

Governments for transfers of population, e.g. the expulsion of nearly twelve million Germans from East Germany, Czechoslovakia and other countries to West Germany between 1945 and 1950.

Even more deplorable is the reverse situation of enforced repatriation. Under the Yalta Agreement between the allied leaders at the end of the Second World War, not only tens of thousands of Cossacks and men of the Russian Liberation Army who had fought for the Germans, but thousands of Russian prisoners of war and civilians including women and children who had not, were forcibly repatriated to Russia to go straight to the infamous forced labour camps where many thousands perished. The moral conclusions to be drawn from this dreadful episode are:

(i) a prisoner of war or a captured civilian has a right not to be forcibly repatriated, unless it can be shown that he both fought against his own country and had a duty of allegiance to it;

(ii) states have a duty not to forcibly repatriate prisoners of war or captured civilians not guilty of treason or not owing a duty of allegiance;

(iii) states have a right to refuse to repatriate prisoners of war or captured civilians who do not wish to be repatriated.[19]

The right not to be prevented or legally prohibited from leaving one's own country is necessarily more restricted, since there are many counts on which a state might legitimately impose limitations, e.g. the right of a Third World country to prevent highly skilled or professional personnel taking up more lucrative posts elsewhere. It is possible, however, to indicate where human rights considerations invalidate certain kinds of restrictions on the rights to travel abroad or to emigrate.

(i) Restriction of the right to travel abroad or to apply for permission to emigrate can never be justified when the restriction is applied discriminatorily, i.e. to the disadvantage of persons of a particular sex, colour, race, national origin or ethnic group.

(ii) Members of any group subject to persistent and substantial discrimination with respect to the grant or exercise of human rights have a right to be given the opportunity to go to any country willing to accept them.

(iii) In the last resort any man or woman has a natural right to seek to leave his own country without the permission of the authorities and to seek refuge elsewhere.

(iv) A refugee liable to prosecution for unlawful exit from his own country has a right not to be handed over by the state he is now in to his own state authorities, except where required by those authorities for a criminal offence not itself contrary to human rights requirements.

(v) A person who has been allowed to leave his own country temporarily has a right to return to it.

Freedom of marriage

Today the right to freedom in marrying is regarded in the West as a self-evident right of every man and woman, but forced marriage was until recently a common and accepted feature of Western life, as it is still in some other parts of the world. The Christian stress on the strict obligation of children to obey their parents, and the prevalent commercial attitude towards marriage amongst those with property, resulted in bride and groom being bartered by their parents without their consent in the England of the late Middle Ages and early sixteenth century – children's marriages often being arranged long in advance of their reaching maturity. Where the pressure of parental opinion or the threat of disinheritance was inadequate to secure compliance, physical force might be resorted to.[20] In terms of traditional morality and established practice the right to choose marriage partners was then seen as a right vested in the parents not in the children. Marriage was accepted as existing spiritually as a remedy for sin, and economically and socially as a means of furthering the interests of the family or kin. Even when the emphasis shifted to the interest of the child within a nuclear family the initial result was not the recognition of a right of marriage choice by the child, but a duty of marriage choice by the parents, in particular by the father, for the benefit of the child. The patriarchal rights of the head of the family were exercised by the man as husband as well as father. Though the groom might equally with the bride be forced into marriage, his enforced position was one of dominance. As the great eighteenth century English jurist Blackstone bluntly put it 'the husband and wife are one, and the husband is that one.' When Mary Astell in 1706 cogently asked 'if all men are born free, how is it that all women are born slaves?' a change was already taking place in public attitudes; but that change concerned the conditions rather than the fact of marriage bondage. Though Bishop Fleetwood argued that husbands too had duties, the duty to love their wives, that obligation was seen to derive from a conception of marriage in which wives remained, as ever, duty bound to 'be submissive, subject and obedient to their husbands'.[21] There was to be no equality of rights in marriage, and if it was no longer accepted that husbands had the right to beat their wives into submission, submission to the rule of the husband remained the recognized foundation of the institution of marriage in Western states until the twentieth century.

Just as coercion can never provide a legitimate basis for the contract of marriage, so it is morally unacceptable as an inherent ingredient of the relationship of the parties in marriage. In practice this means that wives, as the physically weaker and socially more vulnerable marriage partners, require legally enforceable rights against being subject to physical injury, restraint or coercion by their husbands. But one cannot be satisfied with a 'no cruelty to wives' position, since this merely places wives on the same moral plane as domestic animals. There is a fundamental objection to women being treated as chattels to be disposed of by fathers in marriage to husbands for their exclusive use.[22]

It is in the realm of marriage that serious difficulties arise with Islamic Sacred Law, where that law is given effect to in a Moslem state. For, although that law requires the husband not to ill-treat his wife, it permits him to chastise her if she disobeys him, unqualified obedience of the wife being the foundation of Islamic marriage. The Moslem wife is also subject to sequestration, being forbidden to leave the house or have visitors without the consent of her husband.

The restrictions imposed by Islamic Law on the rights of married women are grossly discriminatory and severely limit free choice and free development of character. But, as Professor Abdul Aziz Said points out, 'The Western emphasis on freedom from restraint is alien to Islam. While in the liberal tradition freedom signifies the ability to act, in Islam it is the ability to exist' . . . 'Personal freedom lies in surrender to the Divine Will and this must be sought within oneself' . . . 'The goal of freedom is human creativity, but freedom is defined as belonging to the community and participating in its cultural creation' (i.e. Islamic society).[23] It is important, however, to recall that not only was the pattern of male domination and female submission characteristic of Western society until recently, but that its gradual disappearance has been associated with an erosion in the strength and stability of the family. What to most Western eyes appears as mere temporal accompaniment is for strict Islamic adherents a necessary consequence. The 'liberation' of women has brought in its train the subversion of the Western family and if permitted in the Moslem world would destroy the very nature and concept of the Islamic way of life.

In recent years militant Islam has greatly increased its strength and appeal not only amongst Moslem men but amongst women too. Though this is not surprising, given that women are from birth brought up to accept their subordinate position in a society where outside small sections of the middle class this position is accepted as both natural and divinely ordained, it raises a fundamental question as to the status of the human rights of women in Islamic societies. Is one entitled to assert, and if so in what terms, rights which the great mass of people in a society reject as subversive of their particular way of life?

My very tentative answer to this question is that the concept of human rights is grounded in the assertion of the right and the value of all men and women to live their own lives. Such a claim is in fundamental principle incompatible with women being treated as disposable chattels, domestic serfs or sexual slaves, by making them legally subject to forced marriage, or to forced confinement and forced submission to their husband's will on marriage. It is, however, not inherently incompatible with restrictions on the freedom of action of the partners, as some restriction is involved in the very nature of a marriage relationship. Even where the restrictions bear to a greater degree or in a different way on wives than on husbands, a meaningful and satisfying married life for both marriage partners may still be achievable under these unequal conditions. It is essential, however, that the restrictions imposed should be justifiable in terms of their benefit to both partners not one, and that they should not be based on unsubstantiable ascriptions of a lower level of rationality or prudence in women than in men.[24] The question which has to be faced is how far it is possible to bring about the progressive removal of unjustifiable restrictions on women in Moslem societies without threat to the positive and distinctive elements of Moslem culture and way of life.

The right to freedom from coercion in marrying and in marriage has as its reciprocal the positive right to freedom of choice in marrying and in marriage. Free choice in marriage requires the absence of all legal prohibitions or sanctions on marriage between individuals capable of exercising such choice, except those required for the proper exercise of marriage choice or by the accepted nature and purpose of marriage.

The first requires the imposition of some minimum age for marriage. The second restricts marriage to persons of different sexes, to those not already married and those not directly related by blood or marriage. Such restrictions, grounded in long-standing tradition and embodied in established religion and morality, are reasonable requirements. Indeed one might argue that in terms of popular morality the concept of marriage precludes the possibility of homosexual marriages, marrying an already married person or marrying one's own 'flesh and blood'.

More intractable issues are raised by the legal restriction of marriage to 'persons of sound mind', especially since marriage is traditionally seen as instituted for the bearing and rearing of children. In the not too distant past the inmates of mental institutions were kept physically separated·from each other with the express purpose of preventing their 'breeding' hordes of degenerate children. More recent research, however, indicates that the mentally handicapped have a lower than average birth-rate and that their offspring, although below the general average in intelligence, are on average less severely handicapped than their parents. These conclusions lend support to the more enlightened policies being pursued in Western mental institutions designed to make it possible for the mentally handicapped to form emotional relationships with persons of the other sex. The relative success of such policies suggests that mentally handicapped couples in institutions ought not to be denied permission to marry except where they lack either the capacity to understand what marriage is or the capacity to fulfil its minimum requirements, judged by reference to the criteria used in ordinary civil marriages.[25] There can be no case for denying to the institutionalized fundamental personal rights available to persons of the same mental condition outside. The mentally handicapped are persons with rights who, precisely because of their vulnerability and dependence on others, need to have those rights specially safeguarded. But, while all institutionalized mental patients have a right to be protected from ill-treatment or abuse, it is not possible to claim sexual rights for all such patients irrespective of mental condition and irrespective of the opinion of those responsible for their treatment.

If demonstrable incapacity to understand and fulfil the basic requirements of marriage is the only acceptable ground for legally forbidding marriage, it is evident that the imposition of formal barriers to marriage between persons of different races, national origins, colour or religions is completely unacceptable. The purpose of restrictive legislation, like that in operation in South Africa, is not simply or primarily to prevent persons who wish to marry and are capable of marrying from doing so; but rather to sustain at whatever cost a form and conception of society based on racial segregation and white domination. This is a quite different situation from that where members of a particular religious faith are required to limit their marriage choice to persons within that faith, where the penalties for non-observance are restricted to expulsion or social ostracism. What is quite contrary to human rights principles is that the state should criminally punish a man or woman who prefers to renounce his or her faith rather than renounce the one he or she loves.

The assertion of a fundamental right of freedom to marry does not imply an equal right to free oneself from marriage. Marriage viewed as a contractual relationship creates obligations and establishes legitimate expectations for both parties which cannot be unilaterally abrogated – this quite apart from the obligations and expectations resulting from the generation of offspring. Marriage is above all else an instrument of family-creation, with the family seen as 'the natural fundamental group unit of society', embodying vital values and fulfilling crucial social purposes and requiring 'the widest possible protection and assistance' (ICES Article 10).[26] But the protection of marriage and the family as institutions of society cannot be meaningful or justified if purchased at the expense of the individuals who constitute the partnership. The right to be free as a person requires that no party to a marriage shall be forced to submit to continuous coercion and restraint by the other marriage partner, entailing as a minimum an effective mutual right to lawful separation on grounds of cruelty or ill-treatment. Such a right is both morally and practically incompatible with any formal recognition of the right of husbands to chastise their wives to secure submission to the husband's will. It is also unacceptable that the grounds for legal separation or divorce should be substantially weighted in favour of one party. Particular objection must be raised to the provisions of Hanafi Law obtaining in a large part of the Moslem world, which denies divorce to women, except with the husband's consent, while recognizing as valid a thricefold declaration by the husband that he divorces his wife.

The most contentious of all the issues involved in the concept of a right to freedom in marriage concern sexual relations and child-bearing. In individual human rights terms there seems no difficulty in establishing a right of a woman under all conditions and situations not to be subject to forced sexual intercourse or forced child-bearing. A woman's sexual organs and her womb are hers to be used only as she thinks fit and may never be forcibly appropriated to serve another's purposes. The right of every woman not to be used against her will as a source of sexual satisfaction or as a breeding animal is in these terms a right against the whole male world, including her own husband. This approach fails, however, to take account of the nature and purpose of the marriage relationship, which is traditionally seen as existing to create legitimate and sanctified conditions for mutual satisfaction of sexual desires and for the procreation of children. Law and popular morality are in harmony in regarding each spouse as having consented to the sexual consummation of the marriage and having accepted a continuing mutual right to sexual relations. Given the intimate, diverse, and complex nature of marriage sexual relationships it is only to be expected that on occasion one partner, usually but not necessarily the male, will force sexual attentions on the other partner who may acquiesce or put up varying degrees of resistance. While, therefore, one might accept that marital rape, suitably tightly defined, could appropriately be made a criminal offence, it cannot be held that 'forced' intercourse within the marriage bed is no different from forced intercourse without, in the sense that one could reasonably assert a universal fundamental right of married women not to be subjected to forced intercourse, as distinct from a right not to be assaulted and beaten into sexual submission by their husbands. What married women are entitled to have secured to them is the positive right to seek a legal separation, and a negative right to withdraw from the matrimonial abode.

Even more difficult considerations arise where intercourse is used in order to secure the conception of a child not wanted by the other partner. In practice it is difficult to see how a husband could be made to father a child he did not want, since he could always resort to withdrawal or the use of condoms. A wife, on the other hand, may much more readily be forced to submit to intercourse and where necessary prevented from using contraceptives. Since it is the wife who has to bear the burden of carrying the child and giving birth, at some risk to her own life and health, as well as the major share of bringing it up, it is morally unacceptable that she should be forced to conceive a child against her resolute will to the contrary; especially if non-conception can be secured without any refusal of sexual relations. In such circumstances, if neither party can be persuaded to give way, the desired outcome must be secured not by the legal recognition of enforced conception but of divorce and remarriage.

The area of conception is the most private of all areas of personal life and the one above all into which the state has no right to intrude. Far from being entitled to use its powers to force men or women to bear children against their will, the state has a strict obligation to detain and punish any who seek to act in this way. It cannot, however, be held to constitute an infringement of human rights for the state to offer financial or other inducements to women to bear children, provided that such inducements are not designed to appeal to those under age or to the unmarried. From the opposite standpoint there are no adequate grounds for claiming that men and women have a fundamental right to have sterilization facilities made available to them by the state: but there can be no objection in human rights terms to any state providing such a service, as long as the patients are made aware of the implications of the operations concerned.

The most serious infringements of human rights in this area have arisen in recent years from the practice of some governments and regimes in seeking to reduce their rising populations through a combination of force and trickery to keep down the level of births. Thus both in India and China we have seen large-scale enforced sterilization of women, and in China the forced abortion of foetuses and fitting of contraceptive coils. While one may be prepared to accept that no rights violation arises through state offers of inducements to men or women to undergo voluntary sterilization or vasectomy, it is completely unacceptable that men or women should be forcibly deprived of the capacity to bear children. For the state forcibly to 'doctor' men and women, as vets doctor domestic animals, constitutes an unwarranted assumption of power and a gross degradation of persons. Only an extreme situation will justify offering financial or other inducements to ensure the success of state campaigns of voluntary sterilization and vasectomy. In such extremes the political leaders who seek to pressurize the humbler and poorer members of their own communities into denying themselves the capacity for procreation are morally bound to set the example by offering themselves for vasectomy or sterilization.

4

The Right to Freedom of Belief and Freedom of Expression

The character of belief which is claimed as a human right concerns those beliefs which men subscribe to as convictions fundamental to their way of life and purpose in living. Personal beliefs are most commonly expressed in terms of adherence to a specific established Faith or Belief and will invariably exhibit elements which cannot be established as 'true' or 'false', as well as rituals and practices considered crucial to the belief which do not have, and are not seen as having, a truth content. It is characteristic of Beliefs, both that they are the subject of debate, questioning and interpretation by believers and non-believers, so that there will be different views as to what constitutes the Belief; and that amongst believers there are varying degrees of commitment to the practical implementation of the principles of the Belief. To have a belief in this sense is to have a Faith.

Faith may be seen and understood in terms of the outcome of two quite different kinds of experience. The first is faith through birth in a society or a community where all, or virtually all, of the members have a particular tradition of belief or set of beliefs. In the nineteenth century if you were born into a Jewish family in a small town in Tsarist Russia you 'grew into' a believing Jew; just as you 'grew into' a believing Catholic as a Sicilian peasant, or a believing Moslem as a Bedouin nomad. Thus personal belief in the True Faith was the natural outcome of birth and nurture in a society of believers, an outcome which it was the responsibility of believing parents and of the guardians of the Faith to secure. In contrast, faith through personal conviction is a matter of the individual struggling, possibly against parental and social pressures, to arrive for himself at the truth. If the faith he arrives at through personal conviction and commitment is an established Faith he will, as a then-believer, accept its spiritual claims as spiritual truths in their own right, existing quite independently of his act of commitment. But without that commitment there could be no present assertion by him of the spiritual truth of that Faith. If, however, the faith arrived at is an independent set of personal beliefs its force will derive entirely from the individual act of creation or discovery.

These two distinctive paths to faith adherence, through individual conviction *as to the truth* of the Faith and through nurture *in the truths* of the Faith, are associated with two very different categories of Faiths:

(i) Absolute Truth Faiths which assert the requirements of the absolute spiritual truth embodied in the True Faith, overriding competing claims made on grounds of individual conviction;

(ii) Conviction Faiths which assert that claims derived from an individual's conviction as to what constitutes spiritual truth override any other competing Faith claims.

It is immediately apparent that Absolute True Faiths and Conviction Faiths will take very different attitudes in matters of Faith towards members of their own Faith (believers), members of other Faiths (other-believers), and those of no faith (non-believers), and that these differences will vitally concern the right to freedom of belief.

The right to freedom of belief as a liberty right is best understood in terms of individual rights to non-coercion and rights to non-interference.

I   non-coercive Belief rights

the right of every individual to be legally protected against being physically forced to

and

the right not to be legally required, under threat of punishment, to

(i) adopt another Faith or Belief

(ii) renounce one's existing Faith or Belief.

II   non-interference Belief rights

the right of every individual to be legally protected against being physically prevented from

and

the right not to be legally prohibited under the threat of

punishment, from
> (i) adopting another Faith or Belief
> (ii) renouncing one's existing Faith or Belief.

I (i) the right not to be forced or legally required to adopt another Faith
Every Faith will insist that its believers have an absolute moral right
not to be forced or legally required to adopt another Faith and that this
right ought to be legally recognized and protected. But while
Conviction Faiths will wish to assert this same right for other-believers
and non-believers, Absolute Truth Faiths are in a different position. In
their Faith terms it is possible to 'justify' forcible conversion as a means
to secure the ultimate end of universal adherence to the universal
Spiritual Truth which each claims exclusively to embody. Both
Christianity and Islam in earlier times used forcible conversion to
spread the Faith, but the practice has since lapsed and been
renounced. Forced conversion can never be justified in universalizable
moral terms since no Faith is able to accept the right of any other Faith
to so convert its adherents.

**I (ii) the right not to be forced or legally required to renounce one's
existing Faith**
All Faiths will assert the right of believers not to be forced or required
to renounce their existing Faith and Conviction Faiths will assert the
same right for non-believers. With the abandonment of forced
conversion by Absolute Truth Faiths there is no basis for a claim to a
general right to force or require persons of another Faith to renounce
that Faith, since renunciation without conversion to the true Faith has
no purpose or value in True Faith terms.

**II (i) the right not to be prevented or legally prohibited from adopting
another Faith**
The positive right to adopt another Faith raises difficult issues, since
even Conviction Faiths will not accept that a person can have a *moral*
right to adopt a Faith which is morally wrong, whether through its
espousal of morally wrong principles or its devotion to the subversion
of other Faiths. However, it is possible for Conviction Faiths to accept
that everyone should have a *legal* right not to be prevented or
prohibited from adopting any Faith they wish and that the field of
operation of the law should be restricted to the proscription of
particular belief manifestations which can be shown to constitute a

danger to society or to the rights of other-believers or non-believers. There is, of course, nothing to preclude the expression by any Faith of opposition to what is seen as a morally evil Faith.

Absolute Truth Faiths will usually be prepared to take up this same attitude with respect to other-believers and non-believers who wish to change their Faith and will certainly wish to establish the unqualified legal right of such persons to adopt their one True Faith. They will, however, deny not only that any of the Faithful have a moral right to abjure the True Faith, but that abjurers should be accorded legal protection from coercion, intimidation or molestation by members of the Faithful designed to prevent apostasy and may even seek to secure the legal punishment of apostates in states holding to the True Faith. The latter stance is of crucial importance in Islamic states, since according to Islamic Canon Law an obstinate Moslem apostate must be executed.[1]

II (ii) the right not to be prevented or legally prohibited from renouncing one's existing Faith

All Faiths can without difficulty accept the right of non-believers or other-believers to renounce their existing Faith, but only Conviction Faiths can readily accept that their own believers ought to be legally permitted to do so. In contrast Absolute Truth Faiths may well wish to treat the renunciation of the Faith as a heinous act which in a True Faith State should be punished by law.

The sweeping claims made by Absolute Truth Faiths against the liberty rights of belief discussed above require examination to see how far they can be sustained. Thus the Moslem Faith refuses to accept the right of believers to renounce the Faith and adopt another, whilst insisting on the right of other-believers to renounce their Faiths and adopt the One True Faith. Such a claim cannot be morally justified, as it involves treating the claims of other Faiths as completely subordinate to its own.

What this discussion reveals is that, while it is possible to undermine the force of some of the most dangerous claims made by Faiths to enforce Faith adherence in opposition to the principles of liberty and belief, other claims are less open to challenge along the lines developed so far. This is because the universalization principle has been applied to Faiths in their relationship with one another, rather than to individuals. Individuals as believers in Faiths are, of course, deeply concerned with the establishment of rights for their own Faith group since in a very real sense such rights are their personal rights. But in another sense members of Faith groups, along with members of other kinds of groups, must be seen as having rights as individuals *within* the group and in the last resort *against* the group. (See Chapter 5 on rights of assembly and association). Such a conception of rights, as we have seen, is not characteristic of Absolute Truth Faiths; indeed it is precisely the very special nature of Faith as the bond of membership which leads Faith groups of this type to seek to deny to individual members not only the moral right but the legal right to change their Faith. While the right of the individual to manifest his beliefs requires definition and limitation, it cannot be too rigorously asserted that it is the right of individuals, not of a Faith group or a belief system, which must be paramount.

Freedom of belief as the right of individual men and women to arrive at their own conceptions of truth is at the very heart of the doctrine of human rights. Its rock foundation is the unequivocal assertion that no man or woman may be legally denied the right to hold or manifest any belief simply because it conflicts with the fundamental tenets of any established Faith or belief system.

From the assertion 'a man has a fundamental human right to believe what he believes,' a number of principles may be derived:

> (i) no person is morally entitled to seek to prevent another believing what he believes, or to molest, intimidate or injure him because of his beliefs.

The principle does not preclude persons from ostracizing a man of another Faith, condemning his Faith, demanding the legal proscription of particular manifestations or expressions of his beliefs, or from taking action to protect themselves from the direct effects of specific acts of that Faith's manifestation or expression. The principle is universalizable. Its denial entails the acceptance by any person, if the role positions are reversed, of the right of other persons to prevent his believing in his Faith, or to molest, intimidate or injure him because of his beliefs – a position which, while logically just possible, is morally untenable.

> (ii) every state which upholds a particular Faith has a fundamental obligation to give legal effect to principle (i) by:

(a) providing for the legal punishment of those who violate principle (i), particularly those who adhere to the Faith upheld by the state;

(b) refraining from state action in conflict with principle (i), particularly action designed to penalize those adhering to a Faith other than that upheld by the state.

Principle (ii) is universalizable since its denial would, if role positions were reserved, entail acceptance by a Faith-upholding state of the right of another Faith-upholding state not to protect the former's Faith adherents in the latter's territory from personal attack or from legal action designed to penalize them for adherence to that Faith. This position while not logically impossible is morally untenable for any Faith-upholding state. It will be morally untenable even if no other Faith-upholding states are in fact likely to act against Faith adherents living in these states' territories, since principle (ii) is concerned not with the *chance* of reprisal but the moral *right* of reprisal.

The above analysis would suggest that states which are not Faith-upholding states would have no reason for seeking to evade their fundamental obligation under principle (ii) above, though they might be concerned with the impact of particular manifestations of beliefs. Albania, however, affords an unusually clear-cut counter-example to this thesis, since as a militant atheistic state it seeks to prevent all religious belief. It might appear that one could meet the Albanian position by treating atheism as a form of Faith, since assertion of a right to prohibit or punish belief in God would then require acceptance of the right of other states to prohibit or punish those who do not believe in God. This attempt will fail, however, because Albania does not see itself as the upholder of the principles of atheism as such, but only of their own brand of militant Marxism which incorporates atheism as one element, and because atheists at large do not identify themselves with Albania as a True Faith-upholding state. Consequently, whether or not other states proscribe atheism or restrict atheists is a matter of practical and moral indifference to Albania.

What this shows, however, is not that the Albanian case for proscribing religious beliefs cannot be morally invalidated, but that it cannot be dealt with on the narrow basis outlined. It is much more realistic to start from the proposition that Marxism may be treated as a universal secular Faith, embodying a set of truths which it is claimed all men ought to accept and adhere to. On this basis we may distinguish various sects within Marxism, the most important of which are identified with a particular state or states that uphold that particular brand of the Faith. In these terms it is impossible for the Albanian authorities to evince indifference to the proscription by other states of Marxist belief as such, still less to belief in its own 'true' Albanian form. Marxist states are, therefore, required to accept the obligations set out in principle (ii) above, or accept the right of other states to proscribe Marxist beliefs and punish Marxist believers.

One last line of defence is left for those who, without infringing the moral universability principle, want to deny the thesis that the state must refrain from prohibiting or punishing belief. This is to put forward the counter-claim that the state has *the right* to ensure that the True Faith is upheld. But such an assertion, if it is not to fall foul of the obligation already established, must rest on the right of the state to determine what the True Faith is for the community concerned. This is to reduce the determination of the truth of the Faith to the power of the rulers such that if the rulers change, or if the rulers change their Faith, the people may rightly be required to change with them: *cius regio, eius religio*. This is to make a mockery of the whole conception of belief: incompatible with rulers being true believers and unacceptable to true believers. In these terms there can be no place for fundamental rights of any kind, for if the state may rightfully determine what men should believe there is no form or arena of human activity which the state (i.e. its rulers for the time being) may not claim the right to regulate.

Since the beliefs which are the concern of a fundamental right of belief are those considered by their adherents as crucial to their lives, expression and manifestation of belief in some form or other will necessarily be involved in or result from belief. While my 'belief' that it is raining outside may remain in my own head, with no effect on my actions or further thoughts, it is difficult to see how I could hold the *conviction* that the Pope is the anti-Christ without it manifesting itself in some way in my behaviour or attitudes. Manifestation of belief, however, unlike the holding of an uncommunicated personal conviction, cannot be claimed as a right subject to no qualification or limitation. It is to this problem that we must now turn.

The world in which we live is a world of varied Faiths each claiming to embody an exclusive and distinctive spiritual truth. The overwhelming importance attached to these claims has made it difficult for any Faith, especially a universal Faith, to regard other Faiths as other than enemy Faiths, an attitude all too easily and frequently giving rise to intolerance, conflict and even war. Since the reality we face is a multiplicity of competing Faiths and a multiplicity of separate states, some tied to a particular Faith and others not, no possible rational grounds can be adduced to substantiate a claim that any one particular Faith *alone* has a moral right to be accorded Faith manifestation rights under the laws of *all* states. It would clearly be nonsense to suggest that Islam should be accorded exclusive Faith manifestation rights in England or the Catholic Church in Saudi Arabia. The next step in the argument is to establish that no state-recognized Faith may validly claim that the state is entitled to accord it exclusive belief manifestation rights. Such a claim would involve recognizing that all State-recognized Faiths were entitled to have exclusive belief manifestation rights; a position no faith could accept with respect to its adherents in a minority position in another Official-Faith state.

Having secured this base position we may pass on to the more difficult question as to whether some particular Faith or Faiths may legitimately be held to have no rights of belief-manifestation or be denied rights accorded to other Faiths. Claims of this character may be made either in terms of the requirement of the True Faith or of the needs and interests of society.

A True Faith may hold that the case for the denial or a restriction of belief manifestation rights will be substantiated if it can be shown that some other Faith, including any heresy of the True Faith:

(i) denies the truth of the True Faith
(ii) seeks to undermine the True Faith
(iii) seeks to replace the True Faith
(iv) proclaims doctrines condemned as evil by the True Faith.

Claims made in these terms are clearly unacceptable since they might just as readily be made by the Faith or heresy complained of, or by some other Faith altogether, against the True Faith. But it might be urged that to present the argument in this form is to misrepresent it; since what is alleged by Faith x in (i), for example, is not that Faith y denies that the True Faith x is True, but that it denies specific x truths embodied in Faith x, truths which constitute Faith x as the True Faith. It is in this form too that one should understand the objections to Faith y in (ii), (iii), and (iv). What might be held to follow from this distinction is that the objection to claim (i), and by derivation claims (ii), (iii) and (iv), cannot be universalized; since Faith *y* cannot counter-assert that Faith *x* denies specific *x* truths, only that it denies specific *y* truths, which Faith *x* readily admits. However, this defence is less impressive than it looks at first sight; since it is precisely the relative status of the specific *x* and *y* truth claims which is at issue; where there is no accepted or conceivable way of determining whether either or neither is true. Thus, for example, there is no way of establishing whether God exists and consequently whether Jesus is his Son or Mohammed his Prophet. It is precisely because none of the claimed fundamental truths of religion can be objectively substantiated that we have competing world religions each with its universal truths which are truths only for believers, in that they become truths only through or in belief. No Faith is in a moral position to demand that members of other Faiths or no Faiths are under a moral obligation to believe what they do not believe – both because this is a logical impossibility, and because such a claim could equally be made on behalf of any Faith. Since this is so, there can also be no justification for an Official Faith state imposing restrictions or limitations on belief manifestation by other Faiths, simply on the grounds that their doctrines conflict with those of the True Faith.

It does not follow from this, however, that the state must treat all Faiths alike, since this would be to invalidate the very conception of a state religion. What is being argued is that no state is entitled to deny to any religious or belief group the liberty right not to be restrained or prohibited by law from manifesting belief in ways permitted to any other religious or belief group, including secular belief groups. Thus no state is entitled to forbid, as many Moslem states do, one group from publicizing its beliefs and seeking to attract adherents in ways and on conditions afforded to others, whether religious or secular. This would not preclude an Official Faith state making facilities, such as access to television or radio, available to the Official Truth but not to others.

The argument so far has established the following points:

(i) no case can be made in True Faith terms, religious or secular, for denying other Faiths the right to manifest their beliefs;

(ii) no Official Faith state or Government which identifies itself with a True Faith, religious or secular, is justified in denying to any other Faiths the right to manifest its beliefs on the grounds that these beliefs conflict with the True Faith;

(iii) state authorities have an obligation to uphold the rights of individual members of the state community to have and to manifest different Faiths and beliefs;

(iv) state authorities are required to take firm action against the members of any Faith who seek physically to prevent other-believers practising their Faith, or who directly instigate or encourage individual believers to so act;

(v) any case for prohibiting or restricting belief manifestations must be made in terms which are applicable equally to members of all Faiths, religious or secular.

With this base established one may treat most of the remaining aspects of belief manifestation as part of the general question of freedom of expression. There is, however, one fundamental difference between belief manifestation and other-thought manifestation, in that the former, in both its religious and secular forms, is for true believers a necessary condition of life and the vital purpose of life. This is especially true of beleaguered religious sects surrounded by hostile or scornful majorities. It might be thought that in human rights terms all that was required was for the state to protect the members of such sects from outside interference; while recognizing that in practice this might be difficult to secure, not least because some True-Faith orientated state authorities are themselves anxious to wipe out areas of militant religious nonconformity.[2] But there are reasons, other than concern to combat heresy or infidelity, which can lead states into conflict with belief groups. At the extreme such groups may seek to isolate themselves completely from the society in which they are located, denying any obligations to and renouncing any rights in that society. No state can accord to a group, as of right, an entitlement to immunity from its laws and operations. The claims of belief groups which most commonly lead them into conflict with the state may be analysed under the following heads:

(i) claims on belief grounds not to be subject to service obligations to which all members of the society are legally subject;

(ii) claims on belief grounds not to be subject to restrictions to which all members of the society are legally subject;

(iii) claims on belief grounds not to be subject to legal obligations designed to protect the interests of all members of the society.

In the first group the obligations most commonly encountered are those relating to tax payments, military and jury service and voting. Though nonpayment of taxes was the battle cry of some of the militant sixteenth century anabaptists, it is difficult to see how such a stance can be sustained in any but litical terms. No state can maintain itself without taxes; all but the most ineffectual or tyrannical states provide some level of service to everyone; no alternative service in lieu of taxes is realistically conceivable; no clear moral or spiritual basis can be adduced for some members of the community being exempt from the taxes which others pay. A demand of a belief group to be exempt from taxes may justifiably be seen by the state as an unwarranted claim for privileges or, if associated with a rejection of all rights and services, as a demand for secession from the state. The position is different with regard to military service since it is not difficult to appreciate, if not to accept, the moral basis of a claim not to be required to take another's life. It is also possible to see how such a claim can be accommodated, e.g. by granting conscientious objection in return for performance of some other service, without undermining the state's capacity to defend itself. Nor need claimed exemptions on conscientious grounds from jury service or from compulsory voting provide any difficulties, since they can be readily granted to all those, but only those, who can show adherence to a Faith which specifically forbids such activities on spiritual grounds.

The second category is more likely to cause problems, in that a belief group may claim exemption from laws embodying the moral principles of the majority, in particular laws relating to marriage, sexual activity, drugs or use of alcohol. In so far as belief group morality simply permits activity in any of these areas forbidden by law, direct conflict may be avoided by group believers not exercising their moral rights in order to keep within the law. If belief group morality requires believers to act in conflict with the law, the state will be entitled to take steps necessary to secure legal compliance; except in the event that it can be shown that what belief morality requires is specifically permitted in human rights terms, i.e. action which it would be morally wrong for any state not to permit to all its citizens. No state can be held to be under any obligation on grounds of freedom of belief to recognize enclaves of polygamy, incest, juvenile or child sex, drug or alcohol abuse, within its territory.

The third category is the most difficult to handle, not so much because it may embrace such a wide range of requirements, but because of the difficulty of harmonizing the right of the community to act to protect all *its* members, including those in belief groups, and the right of groups to maintain the distinctive way of life which *their* members wish to live. Perhaps the most important point that can be made is that the authorities are entitled as a minimum to ensure that no belief group members are required by discipline or social pressure to remain members of a belief group in which they no longer believe, or to which they no longer wish to belong. There is for this reason something disquieting about closed communities or orders with members subject to rigorous restrictions and exactions, justifiable only if self-assumed, where there is no publicly vetted provision for those who later wish to relapse and depart. The right to freedom from forced labour, freedom of movement, freedom to marry or have sexual relations, freedom to speak and communicate, must be effectively accorded to those who have freely embraced such restrictions. No one original act of consent but only continuing consent of the adherents can justify the perpetuation of community living which involves the denial of fundamental liberty rights.

This brings us to what is, without doubt, the most difficult question of all: the position of children brought up in strict religious communities such as the Dukhobors, Mennonites or Jehovah Witnesses. The fundamental right of parents to bring up their children in the doctrines and practices of their own Faith is indisputable, except where these doctrines and practices are forbidden by laws not themselves in conflict with fundamental human rights requirements. Providing these requirements are not infringed parents are entitled to bring up their children to believe and practise Faiths which others, including the state authorities, hold to be untrue, immoral, or subversive of some True Faith. Every belief group or belief state claims this right for itself *against* other groups or other states and must in consequence be prepared to grant it *to* those other groups and states. Where the sharpest problems arise is with regard to education since, in accordance with the requirements of the United Nations Declaration of Human Rights, more and more states have made education compulsory, at least to primary level, and have built up a state education service for that purpose. Parents belonging to minority belief groups thus find themselves faced with the requirement to send their children to schools which either provide religious teaching in another Faith or provide no religious teaching at all.

It is apparent that as a minimum parents must have the right to withdraw their children from religious instruction in a Faith to which they do not adhere; a right which all Faiths would wish to claim for their members against at least some forms of religious teaching in Other-Faith state schools. But for the more fundamentalist Faiths such a right of withdrawal from religious instruction is held to be inadequate; all teaching has to be imbued with spirit and values of the Faith. Consequently outside teaching of any subject whether by other believers or non-believers is equally unacceptable. The only acceptable solution in such cases is the implementation of the right of parents 'to choose for their children schools, other than those established by the public authorities, which conform to such minimum educational standards as may be laid down or approved by the state and ensure the religious and moral education of their children in conformity with their own convictions.' (ICES, Article 13.3)[3]. Provided that the state authorities approach the question of minimum educational standards flexibly and sympathetically it should, in most cases, be possible to reach an accommodation which will permit belief groups to have their own schools.[4] If, for any reason, a belief group is not permitted to withdraw its children from the state sector and set up its own schools, it is more than ever crucial that no restrictions be imposed on its right to provide belief instruction to the children of believers outside school hours. This is a rock-bottom minimum requirement which every belief group requires for itself and which it must, therefore, accord to others.

Opposition to believer parents opting out of the state education system is more likely to be displayed by militant secular-faith states than by militant religious-faith states, in that the former see education as a means for ensuring that all children become believers in the true secular faith, while the latter see it as a means for ensuring that children born to the Faith are made aware of the tenets and requirements of that Faith. There are other features of secular-faith adherence which make it difficult to assimilate it to religious-faith adherence. Thus, it is much less easy to distinguish a particular area of secular-faith teaching which could in principle be opted out from by those who had conscientious objection to the secular-faith concerned. In Soviet Schools, for example, the whole syllabus is permeated with the principles of Soviet Marxist thinking and consequently there is no way in which religious believers could opt out of alien Faith indoctrination while their children remain in state schools. The case for separate denominational schools is strongest where we have a group of believers whose overriding concern is to maintain and protect their distinctive belief style of life against encroachments of what they see as an alien society, rather than to make that belief the dominant Official Faith of the whole community. This suggests that one might assert a right of parents with particular religious or moral convictions to set up schools for their children, provided that such teachings do not promote disrespect for the human rights of others.

FREEDOM OF EXPRESSION

Freedom of expression lies at the very heart of the concept of human rights in that it is both a crucial end in itself and a vital means to the securing of other ends, including other human rights. The right of every individual to express his or her values, beliefs, convictions, opinions, appraisals and conclusions on the world around is integral to being a conscious self, and inherent in the concept of social intercourse. But although assent to these propositions is easy to secure implementation is another matter. Freedom of expression is commonly feared in that it may threaten the interests and positions of entrenched power holders who fail to justify their power and privileges to the satisfaction of the dispossessed. In particular freedom of expression is a vehicle which may be, and is, used to seek to extract from non-responsible and non-responsive political authorities the human rights which they so spuriously claim to uphold. Once freedom of expression has been secured, in the sense of being actually and effectively asserted, the road is open for securing other rights and incorporating them in the legal and political framework of the state concerned.

Freedom of expression may be exercised either in private or in public. Though private expression may take the form of the individual expressing himself to himself alone, as with Pepys writing his Diary, it usually involves communication between individuals. In either case what is presumed is privacy – the absence of spies and eavesdroppers. Individuals are entitled to express themselves freely in private surroundings without regard to what others may think or feel. Only those who have lived under conditions of surveillance know the terrible sense of loss of freedom which it entails. Since no man would choose to be subject to random secret scrutiny or record, private surveillance to uncover possible crime cannot be justified. Should one, however, accept the right of the state, in pursuit of its responsibilities, to subject to surveillance any person or persons it has reason to suspect may be planning, or actually be engaged in, criminal activity? The answer cannot be an unqualified 'Yes'. Firstly, it is crucial that the possible crimes are unquestionably crimes and crimes of a serious nature. There can be no right to spy on persons who may be planning to do or are doing things which in other countries are perfectly legal or which are protected by, or encompassed within, the framework of fundamental human rights. In particular it can never be accepted that the possible expressing of opinions in private would itself be a crime justifying surveillance. Secondly, just as it is an established principle of the rule of law that citizens should know what the laws are, how they are administered, and what are the penalties for disobedience, they have a right to know on what grounds the surveillance may be authorized and who has the authorizing power. Arbitrary rule flourishes best where procedures and authorities are veiled. No Minister of the Interior or Police Chief forced into exile would willingly go to reside in a country where unknown authorities might subject him to constant vigil for unknown reasons. Similarly no Members of a Government are entitled to authorize surveillance on grounds which they would not be willing to have applied to them if they were ousted from power, or which they would not be willing to have applied against themselves now as members of the Government.

The framework of the right of public freedom of expression may be considered under the following headings:

(i) legal restrictions the state may impose on freedom of expression to protect and secure the legal rights of individual members of the community;

(ii) legal restrictions the state may impose on freedom of expression to protect the society;

(iii) legal restrictions the state may not impose on freedom of expression.

(i) Legal restrictions the state may impose to secure individual legal rights

Since every state has a fundamental obligation to protect the legal rights of any of its citizens against invasion by others, it will be justified in prohibiting persons advocating the invasion of such rights if this appears necessary in order to safeguard the rights concerned. The case for prohibition will be particularly compelling where a group seeks to incite its members and sympathizers to take direct action to deny persons of another sex, religion, colour, race, national origin or ethnic group of their established rights. No group can justify using means of expression for this purpose, since none would accept that others were entitled to act in the same way against themselves. Similar considerations arise with expressions of group abuse, group hatred or the practice of group discrimination of a character which would be unacceptable if expressed or practised against the party responsible by members of the target group. The problem at issue is how to afford protection to those subjected to highly offensive and frightening manifestations of group abuse, hatred or discrimination without seriously restricting legitimate expressions of opinion on inter-group issues and concerns. Since different societies face very different problems in this area, and since the intensity and form of problem will vary markedly over time within any one society, it is neither possible nor desirable to seek to specify universal legal requirements. It is not difficult, in practice, however, to distinguish cases where groups in a society are denied urgently needed protection by the state from substantial abuse, hatred or discrimination from cases where the state uses the claimed need to protect groups from abuse, hatred or discrimination as an excuse for blanketing discussion of harmful or questionable group activities. As with so much in the human rights field what is at stake is not the drawing of precise limits but the provision of effective barriers to prevent gross rights violations.

(ii) Legal restrictions the state may impose to protect society

The second category of restrictions which states may impose on freedom of expression are those necessary to protect the interests of the society as a whole rather than the rights of its individual members. This is a difficult and dangerous area which needs to be tightly confined if individual rights of freedom of expression are not to be seriously put at risk. All legal systems and legal authorities, however, recognize that the state must reserve the right to impose *some* restrictions on freedom of expression where it assumes one of the following forms:

(a) advocacy of the forcible overthrow of the Government;
(b) the publication of information prejudicial to the security of the realm;
(c) the use of public expressions likely to cause disturbances of the peace;

(d) use of public expressions held to be indecent, blasphemous or otherwise morally offensive.

(a) Advocacy of the overthrow of the Government

The overthrow of a Government refers to its ejection and replacement by means which are prohibited by law. Consequently no case can be made for restricting the advocacy of measures which do not strictly fall within this prohibited category. To advocate, for example, that the British Government should be compelled to resign by the mounting pressure of public opinion or by the withdrawal of support by its back-bench MPs is not to call for its unconstitutional overthrow. There is, moreover, an important distinction between stating a general case for people taking illegal measures designed to bring about the overthrow of a Government, and the advocacy of specific action here and now designed to bring about the overthrow of this Government. It is only advocacy of the latter character which may constitute a 'clear and present danger' to ordered government and which may for that reason be considered eligible for proscription. Proscription itself, however, should require substantiation before an independent court that there exists a threat to the existing order of such a nature as to justify the silencing of the advocates of rebellion. All this, of course, is to ignore, as outside the domain of domestic law, the possibility that the overthrow of the Government may indeed be required precisely because it does not permit the possibility of its replacement by peaceful means.

(b) Publication of information or expression of views prejudicial to the security of the realm

In terms of the concept of the sovereignty of the state every state has the right to take action to protect itself from subversion or attack, whether from within or without. In pursuance of this purpose it will claim entitlement to restrict or prohibit the publication and distribution of information which will undermine state security. What cannot be accepted is that the state should have an unqualified and sole entitlement to determine what constitutes a threat to the security of the realm justifying the banning of publication. To do so would be to admit the right of any Government to determine what shall or shall not be the subject of debate, thus undermining the whole conception of freedom of expression. No Government would be willing to accord such a right to its opponents if they were in office. It is vital, therefore, to seek to establish restrictive conditions which must be met before banning can be resorted to, conditions which are themselves open to free discussion.

There are two aspects of this problem of prohibiting publication on security grounds: one concerns the information which might assist those who threaten security, and the other information whose publication might undermine the effectiveness of the security system. In the former area the guiding principle should be that a Government should only seek to restrict publication of material, not otherwise available, which would be of direct value to a hostile power or agency, e.g. information regarding the development and deployment of weapons, location and equipment of units of the armed forces. The public in general, and the press in particular, should be made aware of the kinds of information which it would be an offence against the security of the realm to publish: all other information should be publishable.

The second area is concerned not with information but with the expression of views which might subvert the allegiance and undermine the effectiveness of members of the police and the armed forces. No case can be made for shielding members of such services from the general expression of controversial views, indeed it is vital to the health of the community that members of the armed services should be integrated as far as possible in the community. It is only where there is a direct attempt to subvert the loyalty of members of the armed forces that the claim of a threat to national security can be accepted; since only under such conditions is there any substantiable case for asserting that the expression of view is intended to, and capable of, bringing about a breach of allegiance. Thus in the *Pat Arrowsmith* case the European Commission of Human Rights held that the British Government's prosecution of Pat Arrowsmith for distributing pamphlets to servicemen, encouraging them to refuse to be posted to Northern Ireland or to go absent without leave to Sweden, was not a breach of the right of freedom to express opinions and beliefs. Though arguments might be put forward, and indeed were put forward in the dissenting opinions of several members of the Commission, for treating such actions as expressions of opinion which ought not to be prohibited (since there was no evidence of any danger to security or to order in the army), it is difficult to see how a markedly weaker distinguishing line could reasonably be drawn in states significantly less stable and politically mature than those of Western Europe.[5]

(c) Public expressions likely to cause disturbances of the peace

The same general principles will apply as above, viz. that there cannot be a right of the Government to prohibit any public expressions which it designates as likely to cause disturbances of the peace. The purpose to be served must be the prevention of serious disturbances of the peace, not the prevention of public expressions of opinion unpalatable to the authorities. To this end it is necessary that the persons pounced upon should be the persons actually causing the disturbance (e.g. those attempting to break up a meeting, not the speaker), and that the disturbance does not result from the authorities themselves seeking to prevent legitimate expression of opinion. Where, on the other hand, the views expressed are ones which the Government would be entitled to prohibit but has not exercised its right to prohibit, the authorities will have an obligation to ensure that the form and manner of public expression does not give rise to or provoke disturbance to particular groups in the community. The authorities may, for example, reasonably require marches or demonstrations not to go through or be held in areas where large numbers of such persons live. In all cases involving restrictions on the rights of expression for the purpose of preventing disturbances of the peace it is vital that the decisions reached should be subject to review in independent courts of law.

(d) Use of expressions held to be blasphemous, obscene or otherwise morally offensive

This is the aspect of freedom of expression which has received the most attention in Western countries in recent years, and it is necessary at the outset to insist that what may be the appropriate standards to be applied in such states cannot be accepted as of universal applicability. Instead it might be argued that the overwhelming importance attached in the West to abolishing all restrictions on the right to employ any form of expression one wishes, and the right to enjoy live or pictorial explicit expressions of all forms of sexual activity, no matter how offensive or objectionable these may be in terms of traditional values and moral principles, is a disturbing rather than a reassuring feature of Western life which other societies might do well to eschew. Certainly there are no grounds for asserting that complete or near-complete licence in this area is at the heart of the value and right of freedom of expression: that the absence of freedom in the Communist states is exemplified by pornographic rather than political censorship.

In True Faith states blasphemy is seen as a crime against God and through God to the community of the Faithful; in that God's wrath may descend on the community if it fails to act against blasphemers, since the community exists to uphold the True Faith. What constitutes blasphemy is a matter determined by Faith and the community which upholds that Faith. Such an approach is insupportable in human rights terms, since it may lead to the members of one Faith being punished for refusing to uphold religious principles in which they do not believe. Thus under the Blasphemy Act of 1698 it was blasphemy in England until 1813 to deny the Christian Trinity. Blasphemy laws which seek to protect the tenets of one Faith by restricting the rights of believers in other Faiths to manifest their Faith cannot be reconciled with freedom of belief. Laws against blasphemy may accord with this requirement if they seek to express a society's condemnation of *any* person using expressions of contempt, ridicule or mockery of the doctrines or practices of *any* Faith in terms or forms which will be highly offensive to ordinary members of the Faith concerned.

The difficulties encountered with the concept of obscenity are well exemplified by the fact that in current English Law the offence relates not to the lewd, filthy or disgusting nature of the material complained of (since this is very much a matter of personal judgement and taste), but to its tendency to deprave or corrupt. It is also revealing that the United Nations Convention for the Suppression of the Circulation of and Traffic in Obscene Publications makes no attempt to define obscenity, recognizing that the concept varies widely from country to country.

At the heart of the problem is the undeniable right of every society to protect its culture and values against what it sees as morally corrupt and obscene influences. The danger is that these grounds may be used to restrict free discussion of issues of public concern, or to prevent minority groups expressing unpopular views or espousing unpopular causes. We may usefully distinguish between particular forms of behaviour held to be obscene or immoral and particular literary or artistic expressions held to be obscene or immoral. In so far as the former results in restrictions on public behaviour in such matters as dress, drinking, or sexual activity, or the use of particular words or expressions, it is not apparent that any inherently unreasonable or fundamental infringement of a universal form of the right of individual expression is involved.

With literary or artistic expressions the matter is more complicated.

In so far as the concern of the author or artist is with the act of creation this can be realized in spite of prohibition of publication or display: in so far as it is with bringing his work before the public and attaining recognition, this can in most cases be secured by making adjustments to meet the requirements of the law on obscenity, just as adjustments have to be made to meet the requirements of the laws of libel or copyright. It is crucial, however, that the determination of what constitutes obscenity should be made, not by Government appointed moral censors with powers to prevent publication or display, but by independent courts with power to order the withdrawal of works after publication. The courts should be expected to determine whether or not the expressions complained of actually constitute a real and substantial danger to public morality, and whether the interference or restriction proposed is both capable of averting or reducing the danger and is the minimum required for the purpose.[6] In this way one might reasonably expect the moral censorship involved in obscenity laws to reflect over time changes in a society's moral values and standards.

(iii) Legal restrictions the state may not impose on freedom of expression

The first and simplest principle to assert is that no restrictions on freedom of expression may be imposed on grounds applicable to only some members of the community: in particular that no persons or groups may be discriminated against on grounds of sex, religion, colour, race, national origin or ethnic group, since partiality of restriction is wholly unacceptable in morally universalizable terms. Nor is it acceptable to have general restrictions on speech or publication applied to members of only some groups, when others are exempted or deliberately overlooked.

When we turn to the substance of restriction the most obvious need is to prevent the state exercising powers of censorship, except in wartime. If the right of freedom of expression is to be meaningful it must include both the negative right not to be prevented by the state from saying or publishing things which the authorities do not wish to have said or published, and the positive right to criticize the actions and policies of those authorities. In particular the authorities are not entitled to seek to prevent expressions of concern and protest at the absence of effective human rights and of the demands for their legal incorporation and enforcement. It is bitterly incongruous to see human rights protesters in Soviet Russia being arrested and punished for seeking to draw public attention to the absence of the rights of freedom of expression which the law and constitution claim to guarantee them.

5
The Right to Freedom of Association and Assembly

Man, as Aristotle observed, is 'a social animal, formed by nature for living with others[1]', associating with his fellows both to satisfy his desire for social intercourse and to realize common purposes. In classical liberal contract theory men in the state of nature are seen as having a natural right to form such associations and make such mutual arrangements as they think fit, including the right to make and enforce rules and to punish transgressors. This rule-making power is surrendered when men freely decide to set up a properly constituted political authority; though they retain the general right to associate and assemble together under the care and protection of the state and subject to its laws. Laws, however, may not infringe the inalienable natural rights of life and liberty which it is the purpose and duty of the state to protect. The rights of association and assembly must, on this view, be subject both to the rights of the individuals concerned and to the wider requirements of society.

The rights of association and assembly are liberty rights with both non-coercive and non-interference forms:

Individuals have the non-coercive right to be legally protected against being physically forced to, and the right not to be legally required under threat of punishment to, form, join, remain in or leave any association or assembly.

Individuals have the non-interference right to be legally protected against being physically prevented from, and the right not to be legally prohibited under threat of punishment from, forming, joining, remaining in or leaving any association or assembly.

FORCED ASSOCIATION OR ASSEMBLY

One needs to distinguish between associations which one 'joins' and groups of which one simply 'is' a member, without the exercise of any choice or through any act of compulsion. In all societies one is born into and grows up a member of a particular family, and in some societies one is also born a member of a particular tribe, caste or religious group. As a member of such groups one will have rights and obligations which are likely to be seen in traditional moral terms as irrenounceable and inalienable. Such a view is in conflict with the Western notion of the adult individual as required to accept only self-assumed or legally-imposed obligations. But insofar as natural groups like the tribe are still an important feature of social life in some societies, there is no reason why the states concerned should not accord recognition to the exercise of group authority over those who come within its embrace, provided that this does not involve any violation of the members' fundamental human rights. In these terms it would not, for example, be a violation of the right of freedom of association to recognize that the members of a particular tribal group were required to fulfil a tribal obligation to contribute towards the upkeep of destitute or aged tribal kindred.

Conflict is most likely to arise where a newly-constituted state body intervenes to establish its own authority at the expense of traditional social units, particularly tribal units. Deliberate encroachment of this character cannot be objected to in principle, since the assumption of sole or ultimate responsibility to enact law, maintain order and dispense justice lies at the heart of the concept and reality of state power. What can be, and should be, objected to are interventions directed to securing the destruction of the tribe as a social unit, rather than to the restriction of tribal power and authority to levels commensurate with the needs and obligations of the state. In some cases, indeed, we find state authorities collaborating in or conniving at actions threatening not simply the tribal structure but the tribal peoples themselves. The fundamental duty of the state to recognize and act to protect the individual right to life must embrace a duty towards communities who have over the centuries evolved and maintained a distinctive cultural way of life, which gives rise to individuals exhibiting rare qualities and skills. The fate of tribal peoples like the Yanomami of Brazil and Venezuela should not be held of less concern to humanity than that of the blue whale.[2]

The issues are simpler where one is dealing with formal associations which one joins, since the fundamental conception underlying such association is free and voluntary choice. Only in the most extraordinary circumstances could an association justify taking action to coerce persons into becoming members. One such circumstance might be the collapse of state authority following nuclear warfare and the emergence of localized associations seeking to establish elemental order out of chaos, suffering and despair. But given the continued operative existence of state authority there can be no grounds for any association physically coercing persons to belong to it or to support it.

Coercion of this character is sometimes resorted to by ideological or nationalist political associations which are seeking to overthrow the existing state authority on the grounds that it is the association, not the state, which embodies the will and represents the interest of the people concerned. But how then can such associations justify the use of coercion to drum up support from that population? Two responses are to be found – a denial that any coercion is being used, or an assertion that the coercion reflects the 'real' will or is in the 'real' interest of the people coerced. But the denial of coercion is clearly morally incompatible with its use; while the assertion of a 'real' will to be coerced into doing what one consciously wills not to do, can never provide a justification for that coercion, since it would permit any group to use coercion against anyone for any purpose claimed as the latter's true interest. While one can accept that persons may not know where their true interest lies, it does not follow that those who believe *they* know have a right to coerce those whom *they* believe do not know. Even if it could be objectively established that certain changes in society were in the interest of its members this would not in itself provide a justification for forcing people to act in support of bringing such changes about; anti-smoking groups are not entitled to stop others from smoking or to compel them to campaign for a legal ban on all smoking. But in many cases where political groups use violence in the 'true interest of the people', that true interest is not only rejected by most of those whose interest it is claimed to be, but rests on ideological foundations which are objectively unestablishable or morally questionable. What we have in such cases is a set of beliefs which believers are seeking to force others to accept: a position which is inherently incompatible with freedom of belief (see Chapter 4 above).

The use by associations of non-physical compulsion to secure members has become an important issue in Western countries, particularly Britain, with respect to the negotiation by trade unions with employers of 'closed' or 'union' shop agreements, making union membership a condition of employment.[3] Though the European Convention on Human Rights, drafted in 1950 and in force since 1953, had deliberately excluded Article 20(2) of the United Nations Declaration of Human Rights which provided that 'no one may be compelled to belong to an association,' there was considerable controversy as to whether 'closed' or 'union' shop agreements constituted a violation of the freedom of association guaranteed under Article 11 of the Convention. In 1981 the majority of the European Court of Human Rights ruled that, while 'compulsion to join a particular trade union may not always be contrary to the Convention', the use of threats of dismissal and loss of livelihood against three men who were in employment at the time a 'closed shop' agreement was concluded between British Rail and the three Railway Unions, and who had non-religious conscientious objections to union membership, constituted an interference with freedom of belief and freedom of expression. It is interesting to note that, while the court majority held that the positive and negative freedoms of association were 'two sides of the same coin', the dissenting minority insisted that there was 'no logical link between the two', and that consequently the practice of the closed shop is 'neither prohibited nor authorized by Article 11 of the Convention'.[4]

In the light of the range of opinions expressed within the only existing and effective supra-national court of human rights it is difficult to substantiate that the imposition of compulsory union membership as a condition of employment is inherently incompatible with human rights. The conclusions I would draw are:

(a) the right of freedom of association is not necessarily violated by the legal prohibition of agreements making union membership a condition of employment;

(b) the rights of freedom of expression and freedom of association are not necessarily violated by legally-permitted agreements making union membership a condition of employment, provided that there is no violation of the rights of freedom and security of the person and freedom of belief;

(c) it is incompatible with the concept of freedom of association that a person should be required to belong to a particular union they do not wish to belong to and denied the right to join or form another union which in their view is better able to protect those common interests which trade unions exist to serve. No union can validly claim a sovereign right (whether within or without the union concerned) to prevent workers in a particular 'territory' from exercising their right to form a union of their own by threatening such 'other-union' members with the employer weapon of dismissal;

(d) if persons are required to join or remain as members of a particular trade union as a condition of employment it is necessary to ensure that members of such unions are accorded legally enforceable rights of democratic participation and control, and rights of protection against arbitrary or unfair expulsion.

RESTRICTIONS ON ASSOCIATION OR ASSEMBLY

While only very unusual circumstances and very special purposes can justify forced association, some restriction on freedom to associate and assemble is always required to protect the interests of members of the society. Even with private self-regarding associations or assemblies it will be necessary to protect the basic rights of members against each other as well as the rights of outsiders against unintended, adverse consequences of insider action.

The origin of the right of association is the right of any two or more individuals to come together and set up a private association for any legitimate purpose. An association comes into being through an agreement between specific individuals: there is no question of any individual having a *right* to be associated with any of his fellows. It will always be open to those involved in preliminary discussions about forming an association to exclude anyone from the projected association. There can be no right to be associated together with other persons against their will. It follows from this that no one can have an inherent right to join an existing association. Those who initiate an association have a right to lay down who else, if anyone, shall be entitled to join, and if so on what terms and conditions, terms and conditions which may be different from those of the original members. But what if those associations make the holding of certain beliefs, or the not-holding of certain beliefs, a condition of membership? Does this not constitute a denial of the right of freedom of belief? The answer is 'No', provided the membership of the society is voluntary, and provided that the purpose of the association is not to put those holding or not holding certain beliefs in a seriously disadvantaged position. An association needs to exclude from membership those whose aims and beliefs are contrary to those which the association exists to realize. Such an exclusion causes no major problems as long as those excluded have the legal right to form a separate, possibly competing, association of their own. Similarly membership of an association may well involve some limitation on the exercise of the right to freedom of expression – public attacks on the association, its policy, activities or leaders may be held incompatible with continued membership. But provided that the association does not use force or threats to secure silence, all that one stands to lose by refusal to accept these restrictions are the advantages of continued membership.

It is inherent in the nature of voluntary associations that the members give up part of their individual freedom of action in order to realize certain purposes with each person sees himself as having in common with his fellows. In particular each assumes obligations to his fellow members and to the association under the terms of its rules and in furtherance of its purposes. It is vital, therefore, that a person invited or permitted to join an association should know what obligations he is assuming under its rules and procedures, and what purposes it seeks to further. Each new member has along with each existing member a quasi-legal right to expect the association's rules and procedures to be adhered to, including those related to the members' rights of resignation and the association's rights of expulsion. In the case of dispute over rules and procedures both the association and its members should have a legal right of access to the courts to settle the points at issue. The law and the courts will be responsible for ensuring that neither an association's rules nor its actions involve any violation of the fundamental human rights of the members. In particular no association has a right to impose obligations or penalties on members, would-be members, or members who wish to resign, which involve the use or threat of physical violence against the members or their families. This will be so even if the members concerned originally consented to the imposition of such obligations and penalties as a condition of membership.

The position is rather different where one is dealing with associations which open their membership to the public at large, or to particular sections of the public. Public associations fall into two broad categories, interest groups and cause-promotional groups. Some interest groups, like the trade unions, are large and influential and may confer very considerable benefits on their members. It is, therefore, reasonable to expect that membership should be open to all who naturally fall within the field of the interest concerned. There are strong objections to the deliberate exclusion of persons on grounds of race, colour, ethnic group or national origin, religion or sex where exclusion is practised by the privileged against the underprivileged; since the association then operates as an instrument to keep the underprivileged in their subordinate place and depressed condition. Members of the all-white miners' union in South Africa, for example, paid many times the wages received by black miners, would not be willing to accept a reversal of the situation whereby they were excluded from an all-black union, if the blacks had under an African majority Government the wages and privileges the whites now enjoy, and the whites 'enjoyed' black conditions and wages. It will be legitimate, therefore, for the state to legislate to prevent dominant group discrimination in the membership of interest group associations. With cause groups, on the other hand, there will in most cases be a strong incentive to seek to rally everyone and anyone to the cause, except where the cause espoused is the furtherance of discrimination, a purpose which may be held to be legally unacceptable.

Restrictions on the rights of freedom of association and assembly may be considered under the following headings:

(i) legal restrictions the state may impose on freedom of association and assembly to protect and secure the legal rights of individual members of the community;

(ii) legal restrictions the state may impose on freedom of association and assembly to protect society;

(iii) legal restrictions the state may not impose or permit on freedom of association and assembly.

(i) Legal restrictions the state may impose to protect individual rights
The first set of questions which require consideration are those stemming from discriminatory practices of associations with regard to membership, or from action designed to prevent members of particular groups from exercising their rights (including the right of association), or from the expression of group abuse, group hatred or

the practice of group discrimination which would be unacceptable if expressed or practised against the association responsible by associated members of the target group. Before turning to the substance of these questions it is necessary to raise the prior issue as to whether such questions ought not to be examined from the standpoint that United Nations requirements with regard to discrimination are mandatory not permissive as far as state counter-action is concerned. Thus the International Convention on the Elimination of All Forms of Racial Discrimination, 1966, requires States Parties to 'declare illegal and prohibit organizations, and also organized and all other propaganda activities, which promote and incite racial discrimination, and shall recognise participation in such organisations or activities as an offence punishable by law ' (Article 4).[5] The European Commission on Human Rights in *J. Glimmerveen and J. Hagenbeek v. the Netherlands* (1980)[6] held that the Netherlands authorities would, if they had allowed the applicants to proclaim freely and without penalty their racialist ideas, have encouraged the discrimination prohibited by the European Conventions on Human Rights and the International Convention on the Elimination of all Forms of Racial Discrimination to which the Netherlands adhered. It used this arguement to support its ruling against the applicants. It is not to be assumed, however, that it would have sought to require the Netherlands to ban the spread of racist doctrines or to forbid the nomination of racist candidates by a racist association. Thus to put the issue in a British context it would almost certainly be the view of the European Commission and Court of Human Rights that it is a matter for the British Government to decide what restrictions, if any, it should impose on the National Front. Except in an extreme case where a British Government actually directly encouraged and supported racism, it should be left to that Government to determine whether a greater threat to the rights and freedoms of British society would be posed by legal proscription of National Front activities or by leaving them subject only to the ordinary criminal law.

If legal restriction is thought necessary a stronger and more acceptable case can normally be made for banning particular manifestations of discrimination by an association than for banning the association itself. Thus it clearly makes better sense to require a trade union practising discrimination in its recruitment to open its membership to persons of all races, than to ban the union concerned. In most cases it will be more appropriate to ban the advocacy of discriminatory action or the expression of group hatred by an association than to require the association's disbandment, except where such racial advocacy or expression constitutes the fundamental purpose of the association.

(ii) Legal restrictions the state may impose to protect society

Associations existing within the framework of state power must accept the limitations inherent in that power. Thus no association may seek to exercise the basic function of state law-making, law enforcing, law-breaker punishing or war-making, except in conditions of extreme emergency where the authority of the state has collapsed, or where the state either permits or itself perpetuates actions against the members of a group involving the flagrant violation of their most fundamental rights. No association would be prepared to accept the right of any other association to seek to take over the functions and exercise the military and police powers of the state. The state for its part has a duty to seek to frustrate the formation or operation of associations, like the Mafia, devoted to the pursuit of criminal activities and to ensure that they do not threaten public order and the basic rights of members of the community. It is also vital, however, that the state authorities should themselves refrain from actions which give rise to or fuel disturbances, and from exercising partiality as between different groups of peace-disturbers.

The International Covenants on Human Rights recognize the right of the state to require that certain categories of public employees should not be members of particular associations on the ground that such membership is incompatible with the proper and impartial carrying out of their official duties. Thus, for example, a case can be made in public interest terms for barring members of the armed forces, police, judiciary and higher civil service from belonging to any political party, or trade union with strike powers or a political affiliation. But no case can be made for banning them from belonging to an association to protect their interests.

More controversial issues arise with regard to whether the state is entitled to ban associations which are held to be morally offensive by most members of a society. The first point to stress is that 'moral offensiveness' may not be used as a reason or justification for banning associations simply because they express beliefs incompatible with, or in opposition to, the dominant belief system in a society. The moral offence must lie in the objectionable nature of the doctrines or practices concerned. The charge of moral offensiveness is most commonly made with regard to sexual behaviour, in particular with reference to adultery, prostitution, homosexuality, paedophilia and incest. Since the majority of persons in almost all societies hold these forms of sexual activity to be morally objectionable or undesirable, and since social and moral grounds may be adduced in favour of either their discouragement or prohibition, the state may reasonably act to restrict associations directed to their furtherance. Thus it may on grounds of public morality seek to prevent the formation or use of associations to facilitate or promote wife-swapping, to prohibit prostitutes, individually or collectively, advertising their services and wares or homosexuals promoting their alternative sexual life-style. On the other hand, it would be difficult in liberty right terms for a state to justify prohibition of associations advocating the removal of penal sanctions against those who engage in prostitution or homosexuality. The same would not necessarily be true of associations to legalize incest or paedophilia, in view of the particularly obnoxious and corrupting nature of the activity concerned. But one is bound to recognize that what constitutes morally offensive behaviour not only varies widely from one society to another, but that such variation is in wide measure acceptable in moral terms provided that it does not involve flagrant violation of fundamental rights.

(iii) Legal restrictions the state may not impose

The central requirement, derived directly from the concept of the right of freedom of association itself, is that the state should not seek to determine what associations or assemblies exist or what their form, principles and activities should be. To have the right to associate in state-established and state-directed associations is to have, at best, the negative right not to belong, instead of the positive right to form or join associations of one's own choice and making. The fundamental principle lying behind the right of association is the freedom to set up any association for any purpose, subject only to the aims and activities of the association not being forbidden by state law, where that law is not itself in conflict with human rights requirements. There is a tight correlation between the existence of an effective right of association and assembly, exercising the associated right of freedom of expression, and the general recognition and protection of other fundamental human rights. This is not surprising, since without effective and operative rights of association, assembly and expression, and in particular without free trade unions armed with the strike weapon, there is no possibility of taking action to draw attention to and secure redress for the invasion of other rights.

In all countries there are violations of human rights but these violations are most common and serious precisely in those countries which prevent men and women acting together in associations of their own choosing to realize their common purposes. No Government is entitled to restrict the right of association and assembly to ensure that its own actions, policies and personnel are not open to criticism or public pressure. Where no such criticism or pressure is to be found in legally recognized associations, and those bodies which express criticism or seek to exert pressure are legally proscribed or subject to surveillance, hindrance or repression, we have clear evidence of the violation of the right of association and assembly and strong reason for expecting to find violations of other rights.

6
The Right to Property

'The natural and imprescriptible', the 'inviolable and sacred' right of property proclaimed in the 1789 French Declaration of the Rights of Man is a personal, private property right: 'the right of property is that which belongs to every citizen of enjoying and disposing as he will of his goods and revenues, of the fruits of his work and industry.' (Article 16, French Constitution of 1793). Expressed in such unqualified terms the Declaration and Constitution were, and were meant to be, a challenge to the principles and values which underpinned the traditional order, now to be replaced by new universal principles and values based on reason and equality.

The traditional Christian conception of property held that God had given man *dominium* over the earth, its fruits and its creatures to use, that God's purposes for man might be fulfilled. Private property was neither ordained by God nor required by Natural Law, but followed from the Fall from Grace and the institution of human law. Private property rights were not contrary to Natural Law, but were subject to the overriding requirements of *dominium naturale* that the earth and its products be used to sustain the lives of all mankind. John Locke, though often seen as the spiritual father of the inviolable and sacred rights of private property, remained firmly embedded in the older tradition. 'God the Lord and Father of all, has given no one of his Children such a Property; in his peculiar Portion of the things of this World, but that he has given his needy Brother a *Right* to the Surplusage of his Goods; so that *it cannot justly be denyd him*, when his pressing Wants call for it. And therefore no Man could ever have a just Power over the Life of another, by Right of property in Land or Possessions.'[1]

It was precisely because the long-established and firmly grounded Christian conception was that private property was instituted by man not God, that thinkers operating within the Christian tradition found it necessary to provide a rational justification for private property in terms which did not conflict with the requirements of Natural Law, or with claims derived from the needs of self-preservation. Over the centuries two main lines of argument were developed – that from personality and that from labour.[2] The first of these derives from the concept of the unique value of the individual human personality and the right of each person to express and realize that personality. Such expression and realization, it was argued, is inextricably bound up with personal possessions, both in the practical sense that possessions are necessary for the achievement of certain fundamental human aims and desires, and in the psychological sense that the possessions concerned become embodiments of personality. While this line of argument is plausible, it is not compelling. It runs counter to another long-standing tradition which sees possessions as a barrier to the emergence of spiritual personality and identity. Modern Western man in particular is often portrayed as having stunted and warped his personality through increasing identification of the self with the self's possessions. Even if one rejects the charge that possessions inhibit personal development, one has to recognize that for most individuals personal relations and a free environment which encourages choice and initiative are far more important to self-realization than the opportunity to exercise property rights. Moreover, in so far as 'things', such as books, tools or equipment are required to express and enjoy oneself, it is not self-evident that these must be possessed as one's exclusive personal property, rather than used or shared with others. Even though it appears that in every known society some objects are regarded as personal and exclusive, clothes for example, this does nothing to substantiate a fundamental right to possess every and any thing so regarded. Personal slaves were so regarded in the ancient world.

Finally it is important to stress that in so far as individual possession of private property is held to be highly conducive to the development of an independent, self-reliant personality, it will require that the maximum number of persons should possess such property. Historically property in this sense meant land or a small business sufficient to provide economic independence, which was seen by many writers in the seventeenth and eighteenth centuries not only as a good in itself, but as a necessary condition for any substantiable claim to independent political representation or participation in government. But in so far as economic independence is socially valued it may itself require restriction of private property if the small independent producers are not to be swallowed up by economically larger and more powerful neighbours. The historical tendency of capitalism is, as Marx foresaw, to undermine the independent small-scale producer in both town and country: unrestricted free competition is itself the midwife of national trusts and multi-national corporations, and the gravedigger of small shopkeepers and peasants. It is, moreover, doubtful whether the members of the latter classes, in countries like India where they survive in their millions, can be regarded as exhibiting either economic independence or self-reliant rounded personalities.

The case for grounding private property rights on individual labour or activity appears more promising. Starting from the premise that each man has an unquestionable right to his own body,[3] the claim is made by extension that each has a right to what he creates or produces or appropriates from nature. This principle is then further extended to justify the private appropriation of land wrested from nature. Such a theory had considerable attraction and moral appeal when applied to settlers carving out homesteads and farms for themselves from the virgin lands and forests of the New World. What it completely ignored however was the issue of the very different, but no less real category of rights enjoyed by the aboriginal inhabitants as hunters, trappers and fishers over wide areas of land and water which they did not cultivate. There are no evident grounds on which one can substantiate a right of enclosure by encroachment or appropriation against living communities whose way of life derives from a non-agricultural mode of securing a living from the labour of their own hands.

But just as the traditional labour theory of property as a theory of land appropriation conveniently and erroneously assumes the absence of indigenous peoples and ignores the existence of rights in land other than rights of or in cultivation, so it also assumes a condition of land abundance in relation to settler numbers and ignores the problem of post-settlement claims from new arrivals. Persons shipwrecked on an island where workable land is very scarce are not likely to accept the claim that anyone of their number is entitled to appropriate as much as he can enclose with the labour of his own hands. A system of property rights would be needed, but it could not be based on first appropriation if the preservation of all is to be secured. Such an original position would thus seem to require some system of allocation of land to families on the basis of need, or some form of communal land usage, rather than each being entitled to what he can grab.

But even if the original pattern of land distribution based on first occupancy and land usage meets the preservation needs of all members of the community, this can provide no guarantee for the future. Pressure on resources may come either from an influx of outsiders or from the natural increase of insiders, and while it might be argued that no community has an obligation to the former the same cannot be held of the latter. That is not to say that each new generation has an inherent right to claim a redistribution of property originally acquired through first occupancy. Since human generations are not serially ordered, redistribution would need to be a continuous process and as such subversive of the sense of security so essential to sustain effort directed to reaping the future fruits of present labour. Rather what one has to recognize is that laws instituted to establish the security of property rights have no claim to be sacrosanct and immutable for all time. The justifications which lay behind some original pattern of property rights can provide no compelling reason for their recognition by present sufferers from the bitter consequences which time has wrought.

Labour theories of property are attractive precisely because they appeal to our everyday conception and experience of establishing claims to the products of individual acts of creation. But, while few would wish to deny that some sense of property rights was derivable from an act of creation, it is not apparent that such a right must or ought to be exclusive. Still less persuasive is the argument by extension that, since some forms of property right are justifiable in these terms all forms are. Indeed one has to recognize that original rights to property are liable to change their nature as they change their contours and their size. The right of the newly arrived hill-farmer to the fifty acres of land he fences and clears is of a quite different order from that of the rancho who sets his fences around thousands of acres in the Brazilian heartland, having first torn up the natural habitat and driven out the natural inhabitants, both human and animal. The claim to enjoy the fruits of my own personal labour is not on all fours with the claim to enjoy the fruits produced by those I employ; especially where the established pattern of large landed estates deprives most men of the opportunity to work their own land and forces them to work for others for mere subsistence rates as the only alternative to starvation. The blunt and crucial point that has to be made is that beyond some not readily discernible threshold control of productive property directly and substantially affects other men's lives, whether as power consciously exerted over others or as consequences flowing from property-holding. Such consequences are the proper concern of Government.

Property rights in present-day society require to be embedded in a legal system based on the rule of law, with independent courts dominated neither by the executive nor by powerful cliques to which men may turn for the settlement of disputes and queries as to the nature of the rights they claim. But given the enormous variation in the nature of property rights in different societies, and the powerful and often insidious nature of the consequences which can flow from the exercise of property rights, it is difficult to isolate and define forms of property rights holding which can be established as warranting human rights status, i.e. subject to legal protection but not to legal regulation or restriction. Even if we restrict ourselves to the simple notion of the right of a man to do what he wills with things created with his own hands, provided they do not threaten harm to others, problems still arise. Thus it is not apparent that a man has a moral right to destroy his own works of art which others have come to appreciate highly. The act of creation may properly be seen as something other than a purely personal act once the creation has established itself in the public arena as a work of art. While it may not be possible for the state to prevent the living from destroying what they have come to reject, it may appropriately do so indirectly after death by upholding the right of the executors not to carry out a legal testament to this effect. The very notion of the right of the now-living to have absolute disposal powers over their property after death, without regard to the needs of the then-living is a dubious one. Even more doubtful are claims made of an unqualified testamentary right of disposal of property acquired rather than created during a lifetime. Given the tendency of market societies to concentrate wealth rapidly, and the social costs of such concentrations of wealth and associated power, most societies have introduced some form of progressive inheritance tax.

Further doubt on the claim that property rights are fundamental in nature and concern arises from the fact that, as Richard Flathman points out, it is possible to envisage a society where there would be no exclusive, individual property rights, without such a society necessarily being unjust.[4] Propertyless men and women might lead lives of their own choosing, without any invasion of rights to life and liberty. Instead of *owning* any things they would have *use* rights over such things as were necessary to maintain life and exercise liberty. Such a way of life might exist naturally in small, simple, traditional societies with limited needs, or be adopted in small, monastic-style communities of like-minded brethren. The members of the first group would never have known personal property-ownership: those of the second would have specifically renounced it.

Given the universality of some form or other of personal property rights, the enormous variety of forms available and their social importance, one needs to be highly sceptical of simplistic theories which seek, without qualification, to assert either the supreme value of, or the base evil of, exclusive personal possession. If, on the one hand, property appears 'in some form'. . .' to be essential for any society,'[5] on the other, 'private ownership of things other than the products of purely personal labour seems always to be either less than full or less than exclusive.'[6] The conclusion which may be drawn from this discussion is that it is not possible to establish a fundamental human right to individual private property in terms that one can substantiate as requiring incorporation in the domestic law of all states and capable of being given effect to in domestic courts.[7] For this purpose one would require specific rights, grounded on universally valid moral principles, to particular forms of property and these as we have seen are absent.

But if one cannot lay down that particular property rights in law are universal requirements in all legal systems, neither can one establish that private property rights are morally indefensible and require universal legal prohibition. Even if the rights of private property which it is sought to deny are rights to property as means of production, or property in hired labour, it is far from apparent that an adequate case can be made. Peasant or artisan proprietorship in itself does not readily stand condemned, indeed the attachment of a family over generations to a particular plot of land has often been seen as conducive to the production of reliant, shrewd and spiritually-rounded characters, as in Cobbett's writings, rather than to rural idiocy, as in Marx's. Nor need the employment of hired labour necessarily involve degradation and gross exploitation. If there is no unequivocal moral basis for the outright universal condemnation of private capital ownership, still less are there grounds for asserting that every state has a moral duty to outlaw such ownership. In practical terms the notion of the universal right to have private capital ownership legally proscribed would fly in the face of the whole concept of universal human rights, based as it is on the existence of differing societies with widely ranging cultures and social systems, involving different conceptions of property relations. There is thus no place for a human rights requirement that no man may be legally permitted by the state to have private ownership rights in land or productive capital.

The somewhat ambiguous and amorphous nature of the concept of property, and the differences of opinion as to its value, finds reflection in international human rights documents. Thus, while the *United Nations Declaration* asserts that 'everyone has a right to own property alone as well as in association with others' (Article 17.1),[8] there is no reference at all to property in the International Covenant on Economic, Social and Cultural Rights designed to give legal effect to rights of this character. Article 1 of the First Protocol of the European Convention on Human Rights specifies that 'Every natural or legal person is entitled to the peaceful enjoyment of his possessions,' but asserts 'the right of a State to enforce such laws as it deems necessary to control the use of property in accordance with the general interest.'[9] The same kind of limitation is imposed in the American Convention on Human Rights, 1969 – 'Everyone has the right to the use and enjoyment of his property. The law may subordinate such use and enjoyment to the interest of society' (Article 21)[10]. Both Conventions require that no one may be deprived of his property except in accordance with the provisions of the law, and the American Convention also specifies the payment of just compensation. Finally the United Nations International Convention on the Elimination of All Forms of Racial Discrimination, 1966, prohibits racial discrimination with regard to the right to own property (Article 5 d(5)). These requirements clearly stand in need of some elaboration.

The first point which has to be made is that it is necessary to be sure that the law relating to property rights and the legal procedures used to give effect to such rights are themselves fair and in conformity with human rights requirements. Property rights must both be protected from arbitrary seizure acting in the guise of law, and be restricted to prevent their threatening the rights to life, liberty and security of other persons. Law which affects property rights must be subject to public debate and be open to public criticism and representation by those who feel themselves adversely affected or threatened, whether individually or collectively in association. Consequently, while a state may legitimately on public interest grounds make it illegal for persons to own property of a particular character, there can be no grounds for a new regime punishing someone for having held such property when it was legal so to do. It can never be justifiable to treat property owners as a lower category of being, not entitled to the same basic rights as other members of the community, or sentenced to forced labour or deportation, as happened to the Russian *kulaks* under collectivization. On the contrary, the application of property deprivation must be subject to procedures designed to ensure strict compliance with legal requirements specifically enacted to protect the dispossessed, and providing for legal appeal to independent courts.

The question of 'fair compensation' for legal deprivation of property is not one on which any precise rights entitlements can be laid down; since in some cases it may reasonably be held that the existing extent and form of property ownership is so grossly unfair, discriminatory or burdensome as to justify confiscation. The practice of paying the market value for property publicly acquired is only appropriate in societies which maintain a free market economic system. All that can safely be asserted is that no man may be put into a condition after expropriation, where he is unable to maintain himself or his family. On the other hand, it is necessary to ensure that the device of state appropriation is not corrupted and misused to serve the sordid private ends of rich and powerful men, either to secure unwarranted compensation for the acquisition of their own land, or worse still to acquire from the poor and helpless land which they covet for themselves.

In legal terms the state is the only body which may justifiably deprive a person of any of his property rights, and then only in the public interest. The main role of the state with reference to property rights is to preserve them from encroachment and to punish transgressors. Every citizen is entitled to have his property rights protected against all other persons. Such protection can rarely be more than partially effective under modern urban conditions, but it must be accorded on a non-discriminatory basis, e.g. not directed to the protection of white rather than black property, Protestant rather than Catholic, suburban rather than inner city, the rich rather than the poor. It is a minimum condition of trust in authority that those whose task it is to protect property should not themselves turn predators or act as the protectors and accomplices of predators. Nor should state authorities and agents use state power and patronage to assist the wealthy and mighty in their bid to extend their domains at the expense of those with insufficient resources or influence to hire legal advisers or to corrupt officials. Even given the will it is difficult to devise adequate legal safeguards to prevent the use of wealth to secure power and privilege, but inevitably, it is precisely in those countries where the power of wealth is most pervasive and blatant that the will of the authorities to curb such power is most lacking. Given the tendency for corporate wealth in particular, whether private or public, to become concentrated in ever fewer and more powerful units, it behoves the state to scrutinize the activities of those giant undertakings and to take the steps necessary to curb their property rights in the public interest – the equal interest of all members of the community. It is not only individuals, however, who stand in need of protection against the adverse effects of the exercise of property rights (e.g. poor tenants against rich slum landlords), but the community at large. Thus both the need for protection against water and air pollution, or the ruination of the habitat, and the positive opening up of needed facilities to the public, e.g. to gain admittance to privately owned beaches, lakes or forests, may require restriction of existing property rights.

The right to property, because of its association with persons seeking to assert their power, wealth and privileges without due regard to others, needs to be subordinated to the basic requirements of those others, in particular to the requirements embodied in fundamental human rights. The rights most directly concerned are the rights to life, to liberty and security of the person, to freedom of expression and the right to freedom of association.

Property rights and the right to life
It is a cardinal moral principle that, *in extremis*, a man or woman may, if denied succour by others, take what is necessary in the way of food and shelter without consent. This moral right of self-preservation is incapable of being given legal effect to, rather it overrides the requirements of the law where state relief or private charity fail. Such infringements of the law may be legally punished, but the transgressor has a moral right to expect that strict legal justice in such cases will be tempered with mercy.

Property rights and the right to liberty and security
No person may have property rights over another in the sense of having chattel rights of ownership, to inherit, buy, sell, barter, gamble or give away another – whether slave or captive, wife or child. It is also necessary to insist that no proprietor may claim contractual rights to the labour of others, where contracts are not freely entered into, or

where the conditions of labour approximate to those characteristic of serfdom or chattel slavery. Nor may the state, except under limited and defined conditions, require its citizens to perform forced labour (see Chapter 3).

Property rights and right to freedom of expression

While the main threat to freedom of expression comes from the state, there is in the capitalist world a subsidiary potential danger inherent in the private ownership of the means of mass communication, especially where one proprietor controls the greater part of the media facilities. Government action to prevent monopoly control and manipulation of the mass media for private, political or other socially undesirable purposes is legitimate, provided of course it is not used to replace private direction and manipulation by Government direction and manipulation. The European Convention on Human Rights (Article 10) specifically provides for state licensing of broadcasting, television or cinema enterprises.

Property rights and the right to freedom of association

One of the most unsavoury features of the era of the captains of industry and of thrusting entrepreneurial capitalism in the United States was their claim to treat their huge concerns as fiefdoms within which their own writ was law. Many of these magnates were prepared to use any means, including coercion, intimidation and molestation to prevent workers belonging to trade unions. The simple point that needs to be made is that in purchasing my labour an employer does not purchase me. He has no right to dictate what opinions I should hold or what activities I engage in; nor has he the right to try and stop my associating together with my fellows for purposes not prohibited by law. The rights of property inherent in the labour contract are required to conform to the requirements of the right to association, in particular to the right to form and belong to trade unions.

But if one asserts a right of association for all purposes permitted by law, provided that such law is not itself in conflict with fundamental human rights requirements, it must follow that the possessors or supporters of existing property rights are entitled to associate together. Associations of property rights holders and supporters may use the right to freedom of expression to oppose any limitations or alienation of their property rights proposed by the state or by other associations, including political parties and movements. Persons cannot be denied the right of association by the state simply on the grounds that they own property of a particular character to which the state objects.

But what if the state, in the public interest and without any infringement of human rights, proscribes certain forms of property-ownership, may it then not also proscribe associations having as their objective the reinstitution of these now-illegal property rights? This is a tricky issue to handle. Firstly, one needs to separate out those property rights whose proscription is actually required by specific human rights requirements, e.g. rights in persons as chattels. In such cases the state is entitled to ban associations, may indeed be required to do so, if the activities of the association concerned threaten the security and liberty of those whom the state has the duty to protect from the reimposition of their former property-bound servile condition. Secondly there are those forms of commodity property rights which the state has proscribed because they constitute a direct and serious threat to the life, person, bodily or mental health of *every* person who buys or uses the commodity concerned, e.g. drugs, adulterated food or drink. There can be no doubt that the state is entitled to forbid associations aiming at the removal of these necessary prohibitions, in order to further their sordid financial ends at the expense of direct human suffering. The third category is where the state has proscribed certain forms of property which it thinks are not conducive to the public interest, but where it cannot be shown that all individuals suffer and where there may be genuine dispute as to whether the public interest is served by the proscription. Such instances are likely to be characterized by a variety of practices in different states – some states will forbid the sale of alcohol, others not; some forbid any private individual to own a firearm, others permit it; some states do not make it an offence for a woman to sell her sexual favours, others prohibit it. Where considerations of utility rather than morality are involved there seems no ground for forbidding associations aiming at the removal of the restriction concerned. But where the proscription derives from a moral condemnation of a practice as evil, where objective grounds exist for such a view, and where the combatting of that evil is a central theme of the dominant morality of a society, a case may be made for forbidding the formation of associations directed to securing the rescission of the prohibiting law. It could not, I think, reasonably be held that the proscription by the Saudi authorities of any association aiming at the legalization of liquor consumption in Saudi Arabia constituted a violation of fundamental human rights in that society.

The most contentious aspects of state appropriation of private property rights relates to the appropriation of private land. Where the appropriation takes the form of taking over large landed estates or restricting land-holding to a maximum amount, with the division of appropriated land among the landless and poor peasantry, no problems of principle arise; since the right to property is subordinate to the right to life and sustenance. But what if the state authorities are committed not to parcelling out the land to peasants and would-be peasants, but to socializing it; not to improving the lot of the peasantry but to the elimination of the peasant class? Is a Government entitled to enforce legislation designed to merge all peasant holdings into collective or state farms? Human rights principles cannot provide a direct answer to this question, but they do permit us to lay down two necessary conditions if such action is to be warranted. Firstly no peasant proprietor should be subject to physical coercion, restraint, threat or molestation designed to force him into the collective against his will. Secondly, each peasant proprietor who wishes to remain outside the collective must be left with sufficient land or other resources to maintain himself and his family. The human rights requirements that no man may be subjected to forced labour or deprived of his means of existence cannot be overriden in the name or cause of socialism.

But, since in the great majority of peasant-based societies most holdings are barely sufficient to sustain a peasant family, these two conditions would require communalization of agriculture to be carried out only with the consent of the peasants concerned. The peasants would thus need to be won over by the authorities – a far from easy task given the strong attachments of the peasant to his own holding. The temptation to ignore human rights requirements and to override opposition in the cause of agricultural reform and efficiency is consequently very strong, especially for those committed to Marxist principles. It is not, however, only human rights which are at risk, but the success of the venture itself, if coercion is used where willing cooperation is not forthcoming. Enforced collectivization in Russia involved not only gross violations of human rights, unparalleled except in time of war, but the complete dislocation of agricultural production causing widespread famine in the early thirties, followed by years of general malaise, sloth and inefficiency continuing down to this day.

The thorny rights question which arises from this is whether, because the first generation of collective farmers were forced into the *kolkhozi* against their will, their present descendants on these farms are entitled to form associations to demand decollectivization and restitution of private holdings? Given the doubtful nature of hereditary property rights claims the answer must surely be that a long-past crime committed against the dead cannot justify or require restitution to the present living.[11] It should, however, be open to the living at any time to urge the desirability of changing the present forms of economic relationships and property holdings. If Marxists claim that the workers in capitalist societies are entitled to organize to secure the transformation of private property into socialist property, what grounds can there be for denying workers in socialist countries the right to organize to secure the transformation of socialist property into private property? It is no answer to assert the historically progressive and more advanced nature of the former and historically reactionary and primitive nature of the latter, since this is the very matter in dispute and requiring to be established. Moreover it is precisely those who are the supposed beneficiaries of the claimed higher form of property relations in Russia who show, by their assiduous attention to their private plots and their lack of attention to communal land, where their preference and interest lies after fifty years of this historically higher form of agricultural production. Nor can it be argued, in the light of experience in Yugoslavia and Poland, that a socialist form of society is incompatible with a predominantly private agricultural sector.

But if there can be no justification for socialist societies proscribing associations of collective farmers calling for the decollectivization of agriculture, must this not also apply to those who wish to call for the privatization of other sectors of the economy, including industry? Again the answer must be 'Yes'. Given, however, the social realities of life in socialist societies one should recognize that outside of personal and domestic services and small-scale trading, where a large amount of petty, private economic activity already exists and is tolerated, there is little basis for the emergence of popular associations calling for the restoration of large-scale capitalist productive relations. It is pertinent to note that neither the *Charter 74* movement in Czechoslovakia, the *Praxis* group in Yugoslavia, nor the *Solidarity* movement in Poland proposed the desocialization of industry: all accepted as given the socialist economic basis of their societies. What these movements were concerned to claim was that workers should have the legal right to participate much more directly in the running of industry and that there should be public debate on fundamental questions concerning the structure and working of the economy – discussion which would not preclude the raising of questions as to the appropriateness of retaining socialized property in particular economic areas or in particular organizational forms.

7
Economic and Social Rights

The economic and social rights embodied in the International Covenant on Economic, Social and Cultural Rights (ICES), are often referred to as 'second generation' rights in contrast to the traditional 'first generation' rights of the International Covenant on Civil and Political Rights (ICPR).[1] While the official United Nations position is to insist on the equal importance of both sets of rights there is a strong tendency for Communist and Third World states, who together constitute a substantial numerical majority, to attach greater importance to the former. Thus, while a 1977 General Assembly resolution declared that 'equal attention and urgent consideration should be given to the implementation, promotion and protection of both civil and political, and economic, social and cultural rights', it went on to assert that 'the full realization of civil and political rights without the enjoyment of economic, social and cultural rights is impossible;'[2] a decision which led the nine European Community states 'to reserve their position of principle' on the resolution's implication that 'the enjoyment of economic, social and cultural rights should precede the realization of civil and political rights.'[3]

While many socialists would endorse the view that the satisfaction of economic and social rights should take precedence over the realization of civil and political rights, many Western liberals take the opposite view. Indeed some, like Maurice Cranston, have denied that the claimed economic and social rights are universal human rights at all, being in 'a different logical category' from the traditional civil and political rights; since unlike the latter they cannot be transformed into universal positive legal rights against some specific person or body and cannot be enforced by an international court.[4]

There are two distinct points at issue here: whether the two sets of rights fundamentally differ from each other and whether they conflict with each other. Neither of these questions can be sensibly discussed, however, until specific economic and social rights are analysed, as specific civil and political rights have been. One preliminary point needs to be disposed of, however, concerning the status of the important group of economic rights, e.g. the right to just and favourable conditions of work, which apply only to employed persons. Does this limitation of application mean a lack of the criteria of universality necessary for classification as a fundamental human right? The answer to this is that the conception of fundamental human rights does not derive from tightly-defined, fundamental axioms to which all rights are strictly required to conform. If universality were used as a rigid axiomatic requirement it would rule out, for example, any notion of the rights of the child and the parents, of the accused and the prisoner. In this connection it is pertinent to note that, while general economic and social rights apply to all members of the community, they primarily serve the interests of the weaker and poorer sections. The rich and privileged members of any society do not need any guarantee of a right to health or education, since they are always in a position to secure access to the best available. In human rights terms universality requires that the right claimed is relevant and important to every man and woman in society, rather than that it should be a right which every person is or should be in a position immediately to exercise. Thus, though most people in the West do not practise a religious faith the right to manifest religious belief in worship and observance meets the universality requirement of a human right because it is a right which all men ought to have and which any man might wish to exercise. Similarly the right to just and favourable conditions of work will meet the universality requirement even where most persons are not in employment, if it can be shown that it is a right which all men ought to have and which any man or woman might wish to exercise.

The economic and social rights I propose to discuss are:

(i) the right to form trade unions
(ii) the right to work
(iii) the right to just and favourable conditions of work
(iv) the right to an adequate standard of living
(v) the right to social security, assistance and welfare
(vi) the right to health
(vii) the right to education.

The first three rights are rights of persons as workers, while the remainder are general rights of persons.

(i) The right to form trade unions

The right to form trade unions appears both in ICCPR as an integral part of the right of freedom of association (Article 22), and in ICES (Article 8), which specifically links it with the right to strike. The grounds for asserting a fundamental right of association are dealt with in Chapter 5 above, where attention was paid to the special position of trade unions in relation, on the one hand, to requiring persons to belong to trade unions (the closed shop) and barring certain employees, such as the police and members of the armed forces, from belonging to unions armed with the strike weapon; and, on the other, to the crucial instrumental role which trade unions perform in protecting human rights.[5]

The right to form trade unions is at root a liberty right, requiring state removal of proscriptive legislation and state protection of the exercise of the right. In particular it requires that employers be prohibited from dismissing employees solely on the grounds of union membership. Conversely, as I have argued in Chapter 5, the state has an obligation to protect persons against some manifestations of compulsory union membership. The right to form and join trade unions cannot be exercised in the absence of other basic rights. Thus the International Labour Office at its 1970 Annual Conference listed the civil and political liberties essential to the normal exercise of trade union rights as the rights to freedom and security of the person, freedom from arbitrary arrest and detention, freedom of opinion and expression, freedom of assembly, a fair trial before an independent and impartial tribunal, and to the protection of trade union property.[6] On the other hand, neither ICES (Article 8b), which speaks of the right of trade unions 'to function freely', nor the European Convention on Human Rights (ECHR), which envisages the right of everyone to join trade unions 'for the protection of his interests' (Article 11.1), is specific as to the requirements necessary for effective, free-functioning trade unions. Yet it is apparent, for example, that the refusal of employers or of the state as employer to recognize and negotiate with trade unions may frustrate the purpose of the right to form trade unions, and that the prohibition of picketing will seriously reduce the value of the right to strike.

The former point was strongly argued by Mr Fawcett for the European Commission of Human Rights in the *National Union of Belgium Police Case* before the European Court of Human Rights. He insisted that the right to consultation was not a 'neighbourhood' right, related to but separate from the right of association in trade unions, but an 'organic' right – 'a basic and essential requirement of trade union activity. A trade union has no meaning or effect if it is to be denied consultation;'[7] though he accepted that an effective right of consultation might exist through practice as a non-enforceable 'right by convention', as in the United Kingdom, as well as through an enforceable right by law. The Court, however, was not prepared to go beyond the acceptance of a right of trade unions to be heard, leaving each state 'a free choice of means to be used towards this end.'[8] In this connection it is pertinent that the European Committee of Experts set up by the Committee of Ministers of the Council of Europe under the European Social Charter, 1961,[9] (which makes no provision for judicial proceedings), has provided a detailed interpretation of Articles 5 and 6 of the Charter dealing with 'the Right to Organize' and 'The Right to Bargain Collectively'. Thus with regard to the latter the Committee of Experts has argued that the stated obligation to promote machinery for voluntary negotiations between employers' and workers' organizations requires that the state party concerned shall actively promote such agreements if their spontaneous development is not satisfactory, and to take steps ensure that each side is prepared to bargain collectively with the other.[10]

The International Labour Office's Committee of Experts has informed the United Nations Economic and Social Council, (as the body responsible for supervising the implementation of ICES) of a wide range of issues relevant to the observance of Article 8, including the question as to whether a constitutional provision which assigns a leading or guiding role to a particular political party can be compatible with the right of workers to organize their activities and formulate their programmes as they choose.[11] The ILO itself has published a number of Conventions dealing with the rights of trade unions which state parties undertake to give effect to. Thus ILO 98 requires that employment shall not be conditional on the worker not joining, or leaving a trade union, nor should workers be dismissed or prejudiced for union membership or activities, and that measures 'appropriate to national conditions' should be taken to encourage and promote negotiating machinery and the regulation of terms and conditions of employment by means of collective agreements between employers' and workers' organizations.[12]

What has to be clearly recognized, however, with regard to trade union rights, and indeed to rights of association in general, is that we are dealing with two distinct but interdependent kinds of right – 'the right of everyone to form trade unions and to join the trade union of their choice' and 'the right of trade unions to function freely'.[13] The former is an individual right, the latter a collective one. By exercising the former an individual assumes obligations which limit his freedom of action. The exercise of the latter has as its objective limiting the freedom of action of employers and will have as a direct effect and possibly as an explicit purpose limiting the freedom of action of those who do not wish to join trade unions. This action-limiting effect is liable to assume a coercive form where a union avails itself of the right to strike.

I have examined these problems at some length in my book *The Right to Strike*, where I concluded that the right to strike in the hands of workers and free trade unions, though it may, like the right to vote, be misused, or like the right to free speech need to be legally restricted to protect the vital interests of others, 'remains one of the great keystones of democratic political society'. Union rights serve both as a barometer of the level of human rights existing in any state and as the means of securing the realization of rights denied. But trade union rights will not be secured by the mere absence of legislation denying such rights. 'Free-functioning' requires that unions are not dominated or controlled by others, whether these others be employers, criminals, the Government or a ruling party. Whether union rights exist in practice, as distinct from on paper, in any state can readily be ascertained by reference to whether trade unions can and do take strike action without being subject to repression. The absence of strikes in any state is indicative of a level of repression sufficient not merely to suppress strike demonstrations but any manifestation of independent worker solidarity.

It should be noted that in Western states while difficulties may arise in defining in law precisely what rights union members and unions have, for example with regard to picketing, the major difficulty is in ensuring that the law is complied with in major industrial confrontations. In Communist states no free trade unions with strike powers are permitted, since their existence is held to be incompatible with the maintenance of Communist rule.

(ii) The right to work

As a liberty right the right to work appears firstly as the right to be legally protected against being physically forced to work and the right not to be legally required to work, and secondly as the right to be legally protected against being physically prevented from working and the right not to be legally prevented from working. The former was dealt with in Chapter 3 in the section on 'freedom from forced labour'. The right to work, as the right not to be prevented from working at the job of one's choice, cannot be an unqualified right to practise any craft, profession or calling. It must be restricted to the right to take up any work where one can meet the requirements requisite or necessary to its performance; requirements which do not embody discrimination on grounds of 'colour, sex, language, religion, political or other opinion, national or social origin, property, birth or other status.' (ICES, Article 2.2).[14] I can have no right to practise as a doctor or undertaker but only a right not to be prevented from meeting the qualifications required to practise these 'crafts'. These two liberty rights, along with the liberty rights not to be physically forced or legally required to work, are readily capable of incorporation in law.

The Cocoyoc Declaration of economists, social and natural scientists asserted that the right to work involves 'not simply having a job but finding self-realization in work, the right not to be alienated through production processes that use human beings simply as tools.'[15] This goes beyond the claim that every person has a right to the job of his choice in that it requires the elimination of alienated labour, something unattainable at present in any existing society whether socialist or capitalist. It cannot therefore possibly provide the basis for a rights claim for present persons.[16]

The right not to be denied freedom of choice *in* employment is quite distinct from a right *to* employment, indeed the two are strictly incompatible as legal rights of all individuals in *any* existing society. Thus more Oxford undergraduates want to become journalists each year than there are places in the whole industry. The most that could be guaranteed to each and every person is *a* job, with a negative right of choice, i.e. a right to reject jobs offered plus a right to unemployment benefit until a job offer is taken up. In practice, however, there will always be some persons wanting to work but who for reasons of age, disability or infirmity, are incapable of working or of working effectively. The guarantee of a choice of a job for all 'able-bodied' men and women is a guarantee which only the state can give. In socialist states, where all economic enterprises are state enterprises and all economic activity is state planned and directed,[17] this requirement can be met; but only on the basis of a choice of jobs which for the unqualified is likely to be both limited in range and unattractive in terms and conditions. In such societies there is also likely to be a strong emphasis on a duty as well as a right to work. Thus the Constitution of the USSR speaks of the duty of able-bodied citizens 'to work conscientiously in his chosen, socially useful occupation, and strictly to observe labour discipline. Evasion of socially useful work is incompatible with the principles of socialist society.' (Article 16)[18] Article 209 of the Russian Soviet Federative Socialist Republic (RSFSR) Criminal Code, as interpreted by the Presidium of the RSFSR Supreme Soviet in 1975, provides for 'social parasites' i.e. persons living 'on unearned income with avoidance of socially useful work for more than four months in succession or for periods adding up to one year,' along with systematic vagrants and beggars, to be punished by imprisonment or corrective labour for up to one year. Since it is left to the authorities to determine what constitutes 'socially useful labour' this provision may be, and has been, used against dissenters.[19] Moreover, such persons are liable to dismissal from their jobs, even the most menial, and with trade unions dominated by the Communist party are unlikely to derive any protection from the requirement that all dismissals are subject to local union agreement. Their plight is rendered even more serious by the fact that unemployment benefit has not been payable since 1930, on the grounds that work is available for all.[20]

In capitalist states no guarantee of a job can be given as the demand for jobs in the private sector will be determined by market forces. Since the right to life requires that no one should be allowed to starve, it has long been accepted that those without both work and means had a moral claim to minimum life support. In twentieth-century terms this has come to mean the right to maintenance payments from the state. In moral terms and in public discussion there is a sharp distinction between those unable to work through no fault of their own, those unable to work through their own fault, and those able but unwilling to work. Given adequate social resources there seems good grounds for accepting the claim that persons in the first category should be provided with sufficient benefits to ensure that they and the members of their families do not suffer a significant deterioration in their way of life. The overwhelming majority of persons in employment would themselves wish to be protected in this way should the misfortune of unemployment befall them. The same moral considerations do not apply to persons in the other two categories; but while the second group may be held, as victims of their own foolishness, nevertheless to have a claim on society's charity, the third appear as social parasites well able to fend for themselves and as such without any moral claims at all against society. But is there any significant moral difference between the position of the unemployed penniless loafer and the non-employed rich loafer? Are they not both 'social-parasites', contributing nothing to society and living off the labour of others, albeit at very different levels? But since forced labour is unacceptable in liberty rights terms, except in wartime or other emergencies, would it not be wrong to penalize the undeserving poor parasite by granting him less benefit than the deserving poor while the undeserving rich suffer not one iota? The answer to this is 'No'. The issue of undeserved pleasures enjoyed within a society organized on capitalist lines, whether by the idle or otherwise rich, is a different issue from whether different levels of entitlement may be laid down for persons in different moral categories with respect to particular benefit rights. The proposition that the able but unwilling to work have a claim to the same treatment as the unable but willing is one which undoubtedly would be morally rejected by the vast majority of persons, in the sense that such persons would be ready to have the proposition applied to them if they were to adopt such a stance.

There is, however, an important practical caveat which needs to be made. To distinguish between those 'genuinely seeking' and those 'not-genuinely seeking' work requires giving to thousands of officials the power and duty to determine who may be refused benefit or entitled to only a lower level of benefit, a power which is bound to be variously applied by different officials in different areas of the country. More importantly in times of high levels of unemployment the use of a 'not-genuinely seeking work' criterion is likely to be both harsh and irrelevant, in that it requires thousands of persons, especially teenage school-leavers, to spend day after day chasing after a handful of jobs.

It was the phenomenon of world-wide high unemployment in the 1930s which prompted individual governments and the United Nations after the Second World War to recognize as a major policy objective the realization of full employment. This is most clearly expressed in the European Social Charter Article 1, by which contracting parties, 'with a view to ensuring the effective exercise of the right to work,' undertake 'to accept as one of their primary aims and responsibilities the achievement and maintenance of as high and stable a level of employment as possible, with a view to the attainment of full employment.'[21] But what is the nature of the obligation with respect to the citizens of a contracting state? Clearly no individual right to a job is established, but that does not mean that it would not be possible to establish that certain state actions or inactions constituted a breach of obligation. Thus the European Committee of Experts holds that Article 1 of the European Social Charter would be infringed if a contracting party abandoned the objective of full employment in favour of an economic system providing for a *permanent* pool of unemployment, or if it failed to adopt a planned policy of employment, including special measures to help those at a disadvantage in seeking work.[22] In these terms there is no apparent reason why the citizens of the state concerned should not be seen as having a right to have such infringements removed. The European Social Charter itself makes no provision either for individual complaint or for enforcement, (see note 9 to this Chapter), but it does not follow that no provision is feasible.

In conclusion it is important to stress that, of the various aspects of the right to work considered, only the provision of adequate maintenance for those unable to find work is resource dependent, to the extent that only some states are in a position to secure such a right to all members of the community.

(iii) The right to just and favourable conditions of work

ICES (Article 7),[23] and the European Social Charter (Articles 2, 3 and 4)[24] make provision for four separate rights under this heading; to reasonable working hours, safe and healthy working conditions, fair wages and a decent standard of living. With regard to the first of these the European Committee of Experts, while accepting that what constitutes 'reasonable' working hours for the purposes of Article 2 of the European Social Charter will vary from place to place and from time to time depending on productivity and other factors, holds that compliance will require establishing defined working hours by law, regulation or collective agreement and imposing specific obligations whose performance is subject to the supervision of an appropriate authority.[25] In these restricted terms there would appear to be no intrinsic difficulty in giving effect to the universal right embodied in the International Covenant, provided that one recognizes that the extent of such regulation and the terms embodied will necessarily vary a great deal more between member states of the United Nations than is the case between contracting state parties of the Council of Europe.

It is a mistake, however, to assume either that the enactment of legislation is the key to the realization of rights in this area, or that only wealthy states can afford to give effect to such legislation. Reports made by the Anti-Slavery Society to the United Nations on child labour[26] reveal the need for enacted legislation to be backed up by effective enforcement and by popular opinion. Thus the Report on Columbia stressed that, although the law stipulated that children shall not work during school hours and restricted working to six hours a day, it was found that 40 per cent of children worked a nine-hour day and 25 per cent a thirteen-hour day. Not only private employers but the state itself transgressed the law – in 1972 orphans living in state institutions were assigned to privately-owned workshops where they worked fourteen hours a day. In Hong Kong legislation restricting the age and hours of child labour was so flagrantly violated and offenders so leniently dealt with that the Report concluded that 'it exists only for appearances sake,' resulting from an overriding fear that the use of child labour would fuel protectionist propaganda in countries like Britain whose industries are suffering from Hong Kong competition. In India, with the largest child labour force in the world (about 16.5 million), there are just thirty-nine factory inspectors to enforce even the minimum requirements laid down by law for those industries covered by the relevant legislation. In 1979 it was found that over 20,000 children aged five and upwards worked at Sivakasi, the centre of the match industry, starting at 3 a.m. and finishing at 7 p.m. The bright spot was the Anti-Slavery Society report on Portugal, which in 1960 had reported 168,000 children under fourteen in full employment, but where a two-month visit in 1979 revealed no exploitation of child labour. The Report concluded 'If a country contending with such severe social and economic strains can succeed in eliminating child labour, other countries where children work may lack only the will.'[27]

While accepting that it must be left to individual states to adopt legislative or other measures for giving effect to the right to reasonable hours of work it is possible to lay down certain conditions which every state needs to meet in this area:

(i) priority should be given to eliminating child labour especially in dangerous trades or in arduous work;[28]

(ii) minimum health and safety conditions should be laid down for trades and industries most subject to industrial diseases and accidents;

(iii) an inspectorate should be deployed adequate to regulate and enforce the requirements of (i) and (ii);

(iv) if the legal rights guaranteed to individuals under (i) and (ii) are to be enforceable by the rights-holders, or in the case of children enforceable on their behalf, it is essential that:

(a) workers be permitted to form and join independent trade unions;

(b) non-governmental agencies be permitted to act on behalf of rights-holders;

(c) freedom of expression and publication be available to individuals and associations concerned with the protection of rights.

(iv) The right to an adequate standard of living

It is instructive to note that while ICES (Article 11.1) recognizes 'the right of *everyone* to an *adequate* standard of living for himself and his family, including adequate food, clothing and shelter, and to the continuous improvement of living conditions' [my italics],[29] the European Social Charter, which equally lacks enforcement machinery, recognizes in Article 4(1) 'the right of *workers* to a remuneration such as will give them and their families a *decent* standard of living' [my italics].[30] The European Committee of Experts has argued that the concept of a '*decent* standard' of living must take account of the fundamental social, economic and cultural needs of workers and their families in relation to the stage of development reached by the society in which they live. On this relativistic basis the Committee propose that where the wages of any workers deviate to an excessive extent from the wage paid to the largest number of workers it should be considered as insufficient to maintain a decent standard of living. One would presume that those in receipt of insufficient wages calculated on this basis should have them increased, not to the level of wages received by the workers in the largest group of workers, but to a level that did not deviate to 'an excessive extent' from the wages of the workers in the largest group. Much will depend on how the Experts define 'excessive'.

A relativist stance has also been taken up by the poor countries who understandably reject the view that the ICES concept of an *adequate* standard of living means *for them* a bare subsistence level. But in so far as the continuous improvement of existing standards in poor countries is held to depend on outside aid and assistance, it is unquestionably the achievement of bare subsistence levels which has the first and most urgent claim. What is far from clear, however, is what form such claims should take; especially when regard is paid to the argument that economic development in the poorer states, at least in the initial stages, may result in an absolute worsening in the standards of living of the poorest members of the communities, especially the rural poor.[31] What is patently clear, however, is that developing countries have a particularly crucial obligation not to encourage or permit development (whether by national or multinational agencies) likely to erode seriously the living standards of the poorest and weakest members of the community. This applies particularly to the indigenous communities living off the natural habitat. Whatever else a right to an adequate and improving standard of living may require it undoubtedly denies to any state the right to take steps which deliberately or necessarily result in some of the poorest members in the community being driven down to or below the subsistence level.

The whole question of an adequate standard of living, as distinct from the right not to starve (dealt with in Chapter 2), is bound up with the problems raised by the newly adopted United Nations Right to Development and to a New Economic Order discussed in the next chapter.

(v) The right to social security, assistance and welfare

ICES (Article 9) boldly 'recognizes the right of everyone to social security including social insurance.'[32] The European Social Charter (1961), on the other hand, *inter alia*, requires contracting parties to maintain a social security system and to meet the Minimum Standards of Social Security laid down in ILO Convention No.102, Article 12 (1) and (2); to accord assistance to necessitous persons as of right, Article 13(1); to promote and provide services which contribute to the welfare and development of individuals and groups in the community, Article 14(1); and to take adequate steps to ensure the effective exercise of the right of the physically or mentally disabled to vocational training, rehabilitation and resettlement, Article 15.[33] In 1964 the European Code of Social Security was signed, coming into force in 1968. It requires adherents to bind themselves to accept at least six units from a list of categories embracing medical care, sickness benefit, unemployment benefit, old age benefit, employment injury benefit, family benefit, maternity benefit, invalidity benefit, survivors' benefit; with old age benefits counting as three units, medical care as two units and all others as one unit. For each category there is a strict definition of the class of persons to be covered, purposes covered for and the benefits to be secured. The Code of Social Security provides that 'if the Committee of Ministers [of the Council of Europe], considers that a Contracting Party is not complying with its obligations under this Code, it shall invite the said Contracting Party to take such measures as the Committee of Ministers considers necessary to ensure such compliance.'[34] The importance of the Code lies in the possibility it opens up of making social security rights both meaningful and enforceable; since in these specific terms there is no evident reason why individual persons in a contracting state should not be given the right to invoke adherence to the Code in the relevant domestic court or adjudicating body. Subsequently this could be followed up with provision for reference to a European Commission of Social Rights and possibly a European Court of Social Rights.

But two important caveats must be registered. The first is that social requirements applicable within the confines of the member states of the Council of Europe could not possibly apply to the rest of the world. The second is that the European Social Charter and the Social Code of Social Security, like the European Convention of Human Rights itself is binding only on member states of the Council of Europe which specifically contract to become parties to them. Further under the European Convention of Human Rights Contracting Parties may refrain both from granting permission to the European Commission of Human Rights to receive petitions from individuals and from recognizing the jurisdiction of the court with regard to the interpretation and application of the Convention.[35] The only example of a court whose adjudications are strictly binding on sovereign states is the European Court with respect to Community Law for EEC member states. It is only realistic to assume, therefore, that for the foreseeable future individuals will only be granted access to a supra-national court to adjudicate on their social rights if their own state has specifically contracted both to permit individual applications and to accept such adjudications as binding.

Difficulties relating to adjudication on individual rights claims within the territories of the Council of Europe could easily be resolved, of course, by a simple act of commitment on the part of individual states; but quite different problems arise concerning the feasibility of giving meaningful effect to social rights in the rest of the world. In the East European Communist states the issue is primarily one of political feasibility. In the case of the countries of North and South America, excluding Canada, there already exists machinery in the shape of the Inter American Commission of Human Rights and Inter American Court of Human Rights, set up in 1979 and modelled on the parallel European bodies, which *might* be used to realize the provisions of the American Convention on Human Rights, 1969. That Convention provides (Article 26) for the progressive achievement of the economic, social and cultural rights set out in the American Declaration of the Rights and Duties of Man, 1948. Article XVI of the Declaration reads 'Every person has a right to social security which will protect him from the consequences of unemployment, old age and any disabilities arising from causes beyond his control that make it physically or mentally impossible for him to earn a living.'[36] Within this framework it is just possible, given very substantial United States financial support, to envisage provision for minimum levels of security benefit for a restricted range of circumstances which each contracting party would commit itself to provide, financed in part from that party's own resources and in part from the United States. It is difficult to see, however, how regional arrangements would be possible in other parts of the world. Thus although the African Charter on Human and Peoples' Rights was adopted in 1981, providing that 'the aged and the disabled shall also have the right to special measures of protection in keeping with their physical or moral needs' (Article 18(4)),[37] the resources of that continent are so limited as to rule out the possibility of laying down minimum levels of security benefit which all Africans could be guaranteed. For most parts of the Third World social security rights of any kind will only be secured if the First World states provide the bulk of the funding.

(vi) Right to health care

Both ICES (Article 12)[38] and the European Social Charter (Part 2, Article 11)[39] declare the right of everyone to the 'highest possible' standard of health and specify the obligation of the contracting parties.

But while the European Social Charter speaks of the obligation 'to remove as far as possible the causes of ill-health', ICES restricts itself to calling for 'the creation of conditions which would assure to all medical service and attention in the event of sickness.' The former is buttressed both by the interpretation of the requirements of Article 2. 11 by the European Committee of Experts and the detailed provisions of Part XI of the Europe Code of Social Security relating to medical care; while the latter, in common with all the other provisions of this Covenant, lacks authoritative interpretation or application under the limited supervision procedure of the Covenant.

The first question which has to be addressed is what meaning to attach to the concept of 'the highest possible' standard of health, having regard to both inherent limitations and limitations resulting from the differing character of the various societies in which health is secured. With respect to the former it is evident that the right to 'the highest possible' can never be a right of *everyone* to the 'best possible' available *to anyone* in a particular area of health provision or treatment. Variations in the skills of different health practitioners, in the standards of care provided by different health institutions, the availability and effectiveness of new techniques of treating morbid conditions, will necessarily mean that even under ideal conditions most people will not and cannot have access to the best there is in any field. Indeed it is precisely in those countries where new drugs and medical techniques are being developed most rapidly and extensively that the gap between 'the highest possible' and 'the generally available' will be greatest.

In practical terms the significant gaps existing between the 'highest possible' and 'the generally available' are those between the facilities available to the members of different social groups or of different geographical areas. In all countries the richer and socially advantaged members of society secure better health facilities for themselves than do the poor, disadvantaged members. Indeed the top people in privileged groups within poor states normally have access to a level of medical service, either at home or overseas, commensurate with that available to their opposite numbers in the rich states. The north-south divide does not operate at this social level. Those with wealth and power constitute a privileged international elite for whom the right to 'the highest possible' standard of health is an enviable reality. Outside of this privileged stratum we find great differences between states in the range and quality of health provision available to different groups of the population. Some of these differences, like those between medical services in big cities and remote rural areas, may be thought of as natural facts of social life incapable of being remedied, though they may be alleviated if one resorts to the direction of medical personnel or makes use of expensive mobile services, like the flying doctor service in Australia. In the poorest countries neither of these considerations is relevant since they lack adequate medical resources to direct or spread. Thus while the top ten states had in 1976 under 600 inhabitants per physician, the bottom ten had between 1400 and 5500.[40] Even allowing for the possibility of using less highly trained and skilled medical personnel, and of treating patients in local aid posts or dispensaries, it is highly doubtful whether even a rudimentary medical service can be provided from their own resources by the poor states of the world for their remote rural poor.[41] The rural poor of the Third World are not alone in lacking essential health provision. The urban poor in the swelling slum communities and squatter settlements characteristic of exploding Third World cities, though having readier access to the limited treatment facilities available, are even more prone than their rural counterparts to contract disease due to their highly insanitary environmental conditions. All the evidence indicates that this burden of suffering and ill-health is beyond the capacity of Third World states to remedy unaided.

It would be wrong, however, to think that the maintenance of a high standard of health for a people is simply a matter of economic resources. The United States of America provides a shameful example of the working in a rich society of J.T. Hart's 'Inverse Care Law'. That Law states 'The availability of good medical care tends to vary inversely with the need for it in the population served. This operates more completely where medical care is most exposed to market forces and less so where it is reduced.' The bottom black neighbourhood area in Detroit, for example, had in the early seventies an infant mortality rate as high as San Salvador and over three times the United States average,[42] while in the Los Angeles black slums centred on Wall's the effective rates of physicians to population was one to three thousand, compared with the national average of one to six hundred.[43] There can be no doubt that a high proportion of the United States' poor, especially the black poor, do not have access to a minimally acceptable standard of health, having regard to the needs of the suffering on the one hand and the country's resources on the other. It is the high cost of the medical services provided through the 'free enterprise' medical system, dominated as it is by the powerful monopolistic American Medical Association, rather than the overall level of health service spending,[44] which is at the root of the underprivileged being sold short or priced out of the market. Given the long-standing and well-understood nature of this situation there can be no doubt that successive United States Governments have failed in their obligation to 'assure to all medical service and medical attention in the event of sickness' (ICES, Article 12).[45]

In a rich country, like the United States, it is possible to appeal to the universality principle to establish the moral obligation of those adequately provided for and of members of the medical profession to seek to give effect to the principle that an adequate standard of medical care should be available for all. No middle-class American would be willing to accept that his or her own child should be allowed to go without medical care if, for any reason, they were no longer able to afford medical cover in the case of a grave extended illness. Health protection measures which everyone in adversity would claim from society as a right for themselves are measures which they are morally bound to accept as the moral entitlement of others in similar adverse conditions. Where what is claimed is unquestionably within the capacity of that society the state authorities have a clear obligation to ensure that this social rights claim is met. The extent to which this may involve curtailing existing medical practices is a proper matter for discussion and negotiation. In such a debate the views of the medical profession as to the form and nature of the health service to be provided are clearly of great importance, in so far as such views are directed to improving the quality of service offered to the presently disadvantaged. What cannot be accepted from the members of a profession publicly dedicated to the service of the sick are claims which in effect, even though not in expressed intent, put their own social and financial interests before those of the deprived minority.

Different rights considerations arise in societies which set out to provide a comprehensive state medical service. It is important here to stress the enormous improvement which has taken place in health service provision in the socialist states under state medicine. Before the 1917 Revolution Russia had one-tenth the number of physicians and one quarter the number of hospital beds per ten thousand population as the USA: in 1970-71 the figures were three to two for physicians and five to four for hospital beds in favour of Soviet

Russia.[46] Within the Soviet state medical service there still remain substantial disparities in health service provision between different areas, especially with regard to the number of physicians, owing in the main to the failure of financial incentives to attract and the unwillingness of the authorities to coerce doctors to move to less attractive, remote areas. The Soviet medical system also maintains a right of choice of doctor within its polyclinic system. There are, however, two features of the system which legitimately arouse concern. The first is the allegedly increasing prevalence of *blat* ('presents') to secure *good* medical attention, and the second the existence of special top-level facilities for élite members of Soviet society. Corruption is a feature of all societies but it flourishes most luxuriantly where protected from the light of a free press and free associations.

The privileged state medical treatment for the Soviet élite mirrors the private medical treatment available outside the British National Health Service; but with the crucial difference that in the latter case the issue of private medicine is a matter of public debate and of political determination by a free electorate. What is objectionable about the Soviet set-up is less that the top people secure the best service than that the existence and nature of this privileged service is not allowed to be mentioned precisely because it conflicts with the élite-promoted image of an egalitarian society. A minimum requirement of any state medical system is that no groups or categories of persons shall be entitled to have specially advantageous or privileged facilities available to them, unless publicly authorized by laws which specify which categories of persons are so entitled, what they are entitled to, and why.

Important issues arise relating to the respective rights of patients and doctors with regard to treatment. Thus the would-be patient must have the negative liberty right not to be prevented from going to the doctor of his or her choice, or required to go to some other doctor. For his part the doctor has the right not to have a particular patient forced upon him and not to take more patients than he can handle or has contracted for. The positive form of the liberty right is the patient's right not to be forced to have medical treatment against his will or without his consent, although in this area the rights of parents may sometimes need to be overridden by properly constituted bodies acting in the interests of the child. Special care will also need to be taken to preserve the interest of adult mental detainees from being subjected to treatment against their will, an issue dealt with in Chapter 3.

In conclusion it is worth stressing that the most cost-effective way of improving the health of the poor is through preventive rather than remedial measures – the provision of pure water and sanitation, on the one hand, and mass inoculation and immunization against diseases such as smallpox and diphtheria on the other. Private property rights should never be allowed to stand in the way of the first, nor conscientious objection to the second where the lives of others, including the objector's own children, are significantly at risk during an epidemic.

(vii) The right to education

Historically the idea of a right to education grew out of the traditional concept of the natural duty of parents to look after and bring up their children. Over time the notion of parental responsibility has become increasingly associated on the one hand with furthering the development and meeting the needs of the children rather than with furthering the purposes and complying with the wishes of the parents, and on the other with a shift in emphasis towards formal education as the most important element of upbringing. In consequence today the idea of a right of education is now seen primarily as the right of all children to be educated, where the duty of making such provision available is seen as a duty of society rather than of parents. Indeed, since all children are now held to need formal education, and since some parents out of ignorance or selfishness would be likely not to exercise *a right* to have their children educated, compulsory state-provided school education up to some minimum age has become a feature or an objective of virtually all present-day societies. But education, unlike health provision, is not a service whose fundamental requirements are a matter of objective determination: health requirements being basically the same in all advanced industrial societies. In contrast education is essentially value-oriented and the character of the particular orientation in large measure determines the nature of the quality of the education received.

It is appropriate, therefore, to begin any consideration of the nature of the claimed social right to education by referring back to the nature of the fundamental right to freedom of belief and expression. In Chapter 4 I sought to establish that there is a fundamental right of parents to bring up their children in the doctrines and practices of their own faith, except where these doctrines and practices are forbidden by laws not themselves in conflict with fundamental human rights requirements. This means that parents should be accorded the following legal rights:

(i) the right to withdraw their children from instruction in a Faith to which they do not themselves adhere;

(ii) the right to provide religious and moral instruction in their own Faith outside of state schools;

(iii) the right to set up or choose schools 'to ensure the religious and moral education of their children in conformity with their own convictions,'[47] subject to conforming to minimum educational standards laid down by the state on a non-discriminatory basis.

Of these three rights the second is the most important since, even if neither of the others is granted, it will still be possible for parents to bring up their children in accordance with their own beliefs and convictions. The third raises a number of important issues. At one extreme one might assert that the right of parents to bring up their children according to their own convictions should be an unqualified right without regard to the educational requirements of the state. But to accord an unconditional right of withdrawal would amount to a right not to provide any instruction at all, or only such instruction as served the interest or accorded with the conceptions of the parent. The notion of human rights is one which precludes the use of any person as a chattel or instrument for another's purposes and this applies particularly to the relationship between parents and children. If the right to education is seen as a right directed to and centred on the welfare and development of the child, it cannot logically or realistically be equated with the right of parents to bring up their child as they will and for such purposes as they will.

Society has a minimum obligation to ensure that children are not denied access to education by parents and the most direct and effective way of securing this is to make primary education, at least, compulsory for children and to require parents to ensure their children attend. It is reasonable, therefore, for the state to lay down minimum standards of education which private schools must meet for children during the years of compulsory education. Problems are likely to arise here not with regard to standards of attainment in subjects like mathematics or reading ability, but in those like history or biology where ideological or moral evaluation is important. While there is no way in which such difficulties can be avoided, the existence of freedom of expression and association and of independent courts will reduce the likelihood of the state intervention effectively thwarting the legitimate conscience rights of parents in the field of education; since the onus will be on the state authorities to justify intervention in each case. Even where intervention in the curriculum of private schools is upheld this will not affect the fall-back right of parents to give such private teaching to their children outside compulsory schooling as they think fit. This right of moral upbringing is one of the most fundamental of all rights and as such will override any legal prohibition to the contrary, subject only to such upbringing not directly fostering racial, religious or other prejudice or intolerance of belief.

On the positive side parents may claim a right of access for their children to such public educational facilities as exist. It is unacceptable in rights terms either that specified groups be denied access to particular schools or that only specified groups should be granted such access. Where special schools or special schooling is provided it must be available on an individual non-discriminatory basis, with the case for special treatment being publicly made and debated. In particular there can be no grounds for allocating resources on a discriminatory basis in favour of already advantaged groups. While the educational principle of 'separate but equal', rejected by the United States Supreme Court in *Brown v. Board of Education* (1954), may not necessarily be held to infringe the basic rights to education in some societies, the retention of the 'separate but unequal' principle clearly does so; especially where it underpins a society of unequals based on race, colour, descent, national or ethnic origin, as in South Africa. No member of the privileged group would be prepared to countenance such privilege if the direction of it were reversed – from white advantage to black advantage for example.

In order to move towards equality of opportunity it may well be necessary to devote a higher proportion of current resources to the educational needs of those at present disadvantaged at the expense of the opportunity or standards of the presently privileged. The crunch point comes when it is proposed to give preferential access to limited educational facilities, particularly in secondary or higher education, to the educationally disadvantaged, either by allocating a quota to, or laying down lower standards for, members of such groups. The practice of 'positive discrimination' is adhered to in India with the scheduled castes (including the so-called 'untouchables') and has given rise to strong criticism from members of non-scheduled castes on the grounds that it is a denial of equality of education and leads to a general fall in educational standards. It is clearly not possible to substantiate a moral right to have presently-established educational standards maintained, particularly where any fall in standards results from a policy of seeking to open up and broaden access to limited, higher educational facilities. The most one might perhaps claim is the right of members of the public to be protected against any lowering of entry or qualification standards for professional courses, leading to unskilled practitioners of the arts of medicine[48] and engineering being let loose on an unsuspecting public to their serious detriment or harm.

But what of the argument that positive discrimination violates the principle of equality of educational opportunity?[49] Professor Dworkin in his article 'Reverse Discrimination' has stressed the need to distinguish between the right to equal treatment and the right to be treated as an equal, and argued that it is only the latter which can properly be claimed in respect to entry to higher education. He, therefore, concludes that due consideration of an individual's claim does not preclude having regard to wider concerns of general interest and public advantage held to justify giving preferential treatment to members of disadvantaged groups, such as the blacks in the United States.[50] Positive discrimination designed to reduce the disadvantages suffered by members of underprivileged groups should not, on this view, be seen as a violation of a fundamental right to equality of educational opportunity, but rather as a step towards the realization of greater equality of educational opportunity.

It is important to distinguish between discrimination in favour of presently disadvantaged members of groups who individually have suffered from negative discrimination, or who have been severely disadvantaged, and those individuals who have not. There are, for example, no moral grounds for favouring presently favoured members of the United States black community over less favoured members of the white community simply because blacks as a group were subject to substantial past discrimination. Only present sufferers, not the descendants or associates of past sufferers, have substantiable claims for compensation at the expense of present claimants entitled to be preferred on the basis of educational merit and ability. Race or colour may well be good indicators of the likelihood that a person has suffered severe deprivation, but only the fact of individual deprivation can justify reverse discrimination in each particular case against better qualified candidates. There can, therefore, be no fundamental right of individual members of deprived groups to be accorded educational or other preference solely on the grounds of belonging to a deprived group.[51] What can be said, however, is that individual reverse discrimination on grounds of personal disadvantage is not itself inherently incompatible with the requirement not to practice discrimination.[52]

Finally one must stress the prime importance of content and purpose in education. This finds admirable expression in Article 13.1 of ICES

> . . . education shall be directed to the full development of the human personality and the sense of its dignity, and shall strengthen the respect for human rights and fundamental freedom . . . education shall enable all persons to participate effectively in a free society, promote understanding, tolerance and friendship among all nations and all racial, ethnic or religious groups, and further the activities of the United Nations for the maintenance of peace.[53]

While it has to be accepted that every society will to some degree use education as a means of social indoctrination, in terms of its own values, traditions and interests – indeed Durkheim defined education as 'a methodological socialization of the young generation'[54] – such indoctrination need not and should not make nonsense of Article 13.1. Provided that a society both itself respects fundamental human rights in its own practices and ensures that school children are taught to respect human rights as the rights of all men and women everywhere, education can serve the purposes set out above. This is only possible, however, where freedom of belief and expression operates for teachers, children, students and parents both within the schools and in society outside.

RELATIONSHIP BETWEEN ECONOMIC AND SOCIAL RIGHTS AND CIVIL AND POLITICAL RIGHTS

Before turning to the question of the relationship between these two sets of rights it is worth looking at the relationships existing between the different economic and social rights themselves. Leaving aside the liberty rights to choose one's own work and to form trade unions, other rights as benefit rights are complementary one to another, in the sense that the greater the benefit secured under one heading, the greater the benefit likely to be secured under another; for example, an adequate standard of living and health care are conducive to educational learning. However, benefit rights as services make heavy demands on resources and are consequently in competition with one another; the competition is inherent in a situation of scarce resources, on the one hand, and rising expectations and technological possibilities, on the other. The same kind of competition is to be found between rival claimants for funding within any one benefit service, for instance between preventive medicine and treatment in the health care service. What this means is that any conception of appropriate minimum standards in a particular benefit service must have regard to the whole field of resource-consuming services. The right to form trade unions is distinctive in that as a collective right it has been used instrumentally to secure benefit rights for the underprivileged at the expense of the right of the individual to work at the job of his own choice. It is apparent, therefore, that economic and social rights cannot be seen as a homogeneous bundle of rights which may be compared as a group with a contrasting bundle of civil and political rights.

Much of the argument as to the priority to be accorded to economic and social rights over civil and political rights assumes that these two sets of rights are themselves competitive, that the realization of the one must be, at least in the short run, at the expense of the other. Since, it is claimed, benefit rights are more important to the poor in need than liberty rights, the former must come first – freedom from hunger before freedom of expression. This is, in my view, a specious claim, whose substantiation would require that civil and political rights are either incompatible with or alternatives to economic and social rights. The former case is rarely made, if for no other reason than that those who assert the priority of economic and social rights are in almost all cases signatories of the International Covenant on Civil and Political Rights. Nobody wants to try and make a case for arbitrary arrests, unfair trials, or denials of freedoms of belief and expression. But what of the argument for priority as between competitors?

The first point to be made is that it is the denial of liberty rights, not their provision, which eats up resources, since that denial involves the state in maintaining a large and expensive apparatus of restriction and repression. Breaking-up or running down the police state apparatus would release great reserves of manpower for positive instead of negative work, as well as restoring those convicted of political or ideological crimes to the community. Indirectly, while the effective recognition of the rights of freedom of expression and association might lead to some immediate increase in economic costs as independent and effective trade unions came into being, there are no grounds for assuming that free trade unions will necessarily reduce economic efficiency in an authoritarian society making it difficult or impossible to maintain existing levels of social benefits. There is no evidence of a positive correlation between the level of repression and the rate of economic growth in developing countries, whether communist or otherwise: on the contrary the granting of liberty rights might be expected to have a salutary effect, promoting the exposure of corruption, waste and inefficiency and engendering a more positive spirit amongst the 'liberated' work-force.

A very different but pertinent point arises from the fact that in all states some persons do not get the social and economic rights to which they are entitled, particularly where, as in most authoritarian states, the courts are either politically submissive or corrupt. In these circumstances men and women need to make use of the rights of expression and association in order to seek to secure the economic and social rights denied to them, whether by design or inadvertence. In the absence of such liberty rights benefit rights tend in practice to become discretionary, liable to be withheld by remote bureaucratic fiat or a local corrupt boss. To have economic and social benefits as rights requires that I have the opportunity to exercise liberty rights of expression and association to exert pressure on those who, for whatever reason, deny them to me. Where these liberty rights are denied in law or frustrated in practice I may nevertheless assert my right to my rights. Whereas denied benefit rights have to be extracted from the authorities who hold them in their grasp, liberty rights may simply be exercised in spite of the authorities, although a high price may have to be paid and the outcome may well be defeat by superior power. Far from liberty rights being in competition with benefit rights the implementation of the former is a necessary condition for securing the latter, especially in those societies where discrimination is practised.

8
The Rights of Citizens and the Rights of Peoples

Traditionally the natural rights of man were seen as the rights which each individual had in the state of nature, seen either as a pre-social historical condition or a pre-social hypothetical model. In these terms the rights of man in society tended to be regarded as the rights of independent individuals against other individuals or against society, rather than as the rights which men in society require if they are to be enabled to live their own individual lives as members of a community. The concept of human rights as the rights, both negative and positive, which all men ought to have vouchsafed to them under the law, marks a shift in emphasis away from the former approach to the latter. Human rights remain centred in the concept of the individual in that these fundamental requirements are necessary to meet the common needs of the individual members of the community, where each member is considered as a unique person and an embodiment of ultimate value. The situation is different where every member of the community is considered to have common needs derived directly from some general conception of a communal good or of a communal goal.

If human rights are approached and understood along the former lines no inherent problems arise if particular human rights are claimed as collective rights or if particular collective rights are claimed as human rights. Some human rights, like the right to freedom of belief and freedom of expression, may be claimed and exercised by persons individually or collectively. The rights to freedom of association and assembly and the right to strike, on the other hand, can only be exercised collectively; though any individual may seek to initiate such collective action. The relationship between the rights of individuals and that of the collectivity in these areas has already been explored (chapters 4 and 5). But the most interesting and most difficult problems arise where what is claimed is not a collective right derivative from and consonant with an individual right, but a collective right neither dependent on nor subordinate to a prior-existing individual right. The most formidable claimants of such rights are 'peoples'. It is readily apparent that the notion of 'a right of peoples' is difficult to handle, precisely because unlike individuals peoples are not readily identifiable. Any assertion of a claim to be 'a people' is liable to give rise to dispute incapable of being settled either objectively or by general consent. Since it is fruitless to seek to establish what constitutes a people the only procedure open to us is to examine the specific rights claims made on behalf of peoples; in particular the right of self-determination and the associated rights of development and to a new international economic order.

THE RIGHT OF SELF-DETERMINATION

The right of self-determination is given high priority in United Nations Human Rights Declarations. ICPR and ICES each opens with the assertion that 'All peoples have the right of self-determination' and each requires States Parties to 'promote the realization of the right of self-determination' and to 'respect that right' (Article 1).[1] The United Nations Declaration on the Granting of Independence to Colonial Countries and Peoples (1960) provides that (i) 'the subjection of peoples to alien subjugation, domination and exploitation constitutes a denial of fundamental human rights;' (ii) 'all peoples have the right to self-determination; by virtue of that right they freely determine their political status and freely pursue their economic, social and cultural development;' (iii) immediate steps shall be taken in 'territories which have not yet attained independence, to transfer all powers to the peoples of these territories, without any conditions or reservations, in accordance with their freely expressed will and desire, without any distinction as to race, colour or creed, in order to enable them to enjoy complete independence and freedom;' (iv) 'any attempt aimed at the partial or total disruption of the national unity and the territorial integrity of a country is incompatible with the purposes and principles of the Charter of the United Nations;' (v) all states are required to observe the provisions of the United Nations Charter, the Universal Declaration of Human Rights and the Declaration on the Granting of

Independence 'on the basis of equality, non-interference in the internal affairs of all states, and respect for the sovereign rights of all peoples and their territorial integrity.'[2] The African Charter on Human and Peoples' Rights, adopted in 1981 and operative when ratified by a majority of member states of the Organization of African Unity, goes markedly further asserting both that 'colonized or oppressed peoples shall have the right to free themselves from the bonds of domination by resorting to any means recognized by the international community' and that 'all peoples shall have the right to the assistance of the States Parties to the present Charter in their liberation struggle against foreign domination, be it political, economic or cultural' (Article 20 (2) and (3)).[3]

While annotations on the text of the draft covenants make it clear that 'all peoples' was meant to refer to peoples in all countries and territories, whether independent, trust or non self-governing, in practice the right of self-determination has been held by the United Nations to apply only to peoples in trust or non self-governing territories. U Thant, when United Nations' Secretary-General, was uncharacteristically frank in 1970 when he wrote 'As an international organization the United Nations has never accepted and does not accept, and I do not believe it will ever accept, the principle of secession of a part of a Member State'.[4] Only five states, for example, formally recognized the claim of the Ibo people to self-determination, since it involved carving out a new state of Biafra from the body of Nigeria. The United Nations itself kept silent on the bitter three-year struggle of the Biafrans; whereas in the case of Katanga's secession from the Congo in 1963 it gave support to the Congo Government. If, on the other hand, secession claims are effectively established against the former ruling power, as in the case of Bangladesh against Pakistan, the United Nations can be expected to recognize the new political state reality. Only in those cases where there is overwhelming political opposition to an existing regime, not itself a Great Power, will the United Nations endorse the claims of a 'suppressed' people to the right of self-determination, e.g. the black and coloured peoples in South Africa and the Palestinian peoples in Israel.

It is important to realize that there is nothing necessarily hypocritical or reprehensible about the contrasting attitudes taken by the United Nations to the demands for self-determination made by a colonial people and those made by a metropolitan people. The United Nations, unlike its inter-war predecessor the League of Nations, has strongly championed decolonization as an immediate objective. While European member states have been able to swallow, albeit often only after bitter and costly independence struggles, the loss of their overseas territories, both old and new states refuse to contemplate the break-up of the nation-state itself. Even the clean-handed and level-headed Canadian Government is not prepared to accept that the French-speaking peoples of Quebec have the right to constitute themselves as an independent state. It is in the nature of states that they should seek to maintain their territorial integrity, and in the nature of international organizations of states that they are based on respect for national territorial integrity.

But it is also in the nature of the political process as it works itself out over time that attempts will continue to be made to establish new political units and communities at the expense of existing and recognized state units. Which of these attempts will succeed and which fail will depend far more on the political and coercive strengths of the parties concerned than on the moral strength of their respective cases. The prospects of an independence movement succeeding, however, are far stronger against a metropolitan power which seeks to give effect to fundamental rights, than against one which does not. Indeed one may go further and assert that where there exist full political rights of association, assembly, expression and publication, allied to the right to vote and participate politically, the means exist to secure self-determination, if that is what the mass of the people concerned want. But while the outcome of nationalist agitation and struggle may be a negotiated independence, it is equally likely to be some form of devolution of authority or grant of concession sufficient to blunt or blur the appeal of the demand for independence.[5] What has to be recognized is that just as one must accept that there can be no destiny-ordained right of any state to maintain itself for ever as a political entity, there can be no presumption that every identifiable people must at all costs fulfil a destiny to make itself an independent nation-state.

Claims to national self-determination may be made on many grounds and in respect of many kinds of groups within an existing state. While one may assent to the self-determination of peoples as a general guiding principle, it is impossible to assert self-determination as a right which ought to be given effect to, unless the nature of that right can be clarified. One must, that is, be able to show what a group has to establish to substantiate its right to an independent existence. On the face of it the problem is insoluble, having regard to the impossibility of either defining what constitutes a people or laying down a set of criteria which must be met for a people to establish a claim to statehood. It is possible, however, to clear an area of this entangled thicket of unmanageable, enravelled concepts and interminable, conflicting facts if, instead of seeking to determine the criteria necessary or relevant for *any* warrant of self-determination, one claims the right of self-determination as an unqualified, but not exclusive, right of those people whose most fundamental rights are being flagrantly violated through acts of genocide or gross discrimination.

Any state which deliberately commits acts 'with intent to destroy, in whole or in part, a national, ethnic, racial or religious group,'[6] has unquestionably forfeited any claim it might once have had to the political obligation of the members of the group concerned. Those subject to extermination have the right to more than the condolences and tears of the rest of the world. Action under the United Nations Charter is specifically authorized by the Covenant on the Prevention and Punishment of the Crime of Genocide and might be appropriately directed either to the implementation of the right of self-determination, or to the assumption of United Nations trusteeship.

Where some members of a society with the authorization, blessing or connivance of the state, are denied fundamental rights accorded to others, the members of the deprived group have a right to seek to break away and form a state of their own. The most clear-cut examples of gross discrimination are the denial of equal treatment before and under the law, the wilful failure of the state to protect the freedom and security of group members, the denial of political rights accorded to other members of the community, and violation of the rights of group members to practise their own Faith. Any state authority indulging in mass killings or gross discrimination against a particular people provides that people with unchallengeable entitlement to exercise the right of rebellion. The right of minorities to use force if necessary to secure the right of self-determination is the moral equivalent of the right to popular rebellion against despotic power.

By concentrating our attention on these two incontrovertible grounds for the exercise of the right of self-determination, we also resolve the problem of determining who are 'the people' entitled to exercise the right. 'The people' being slaughtered, terrorized or subjected to gross violations of the most elementary rights are objectively identified by the opposing state authority itself; while the discriminatory acts of oppression serve to create or confirm in the oppressed their sense of being a people 'for itself' and not just 'in itself'[7] which must assert its right to self-preservation.

I am not suggesting that only peoples in such dreaded predicaments can reasonably claim the right of self-determination, but that the absence of any significant degree of rights discrimination and rights violation imposes on those seeking to secure independent statehood a strict obligation to restrict themselves to non-violent methods of political struggle. In particular there can never be grounds for any political group claiming a sacred right to engage in armed struggle against the state to secure self-determination and independence on behalf of a people who have themselves freely and clearly demonstrated their unreadiness to seek independence. Even where a people wish to be accorded self-government by the ruling power, they may still prefer the familiar path of dependence rather than the hazardous and tortuous path of bloody struggle to a doubtful independence. No Nationalist élite group can assert an historic entitlement to act on behalf of or to embody the real will of a people who refuse to see themselves in the nationalist image conjured up by their would-be leaders and rulers.

THE RIGHT TO DEVELOPMENT AND TO A NEW INTERNATIONAL ECONOMIC ORDER

In 1974 the United Nations General Assembly adopted a Declaration on the need to establish a new international economic order designed to redress the inequalities and injustices between the richer and poorer nations of the world. The realization of such a new order, involving active assistance to developing countries, was seen as 'an essential element for the effective promotion of human rights and fundamental freedoms,' in particular of economic, social and cultural rights in developing countries.[8] In 1981 the General Assembly took the matter a stage further when by 135 votes to 1 (the USA), with 13 abstentions, it adopted a resolution declaring the right to development to be an 'inalienable human right'.[9] Prior to these declarations the right to development had existed implicitly in international law, and explicitly in ICPR and ICES, as a negative liberty right of non-interference by outside states or bodies.[10] This approach found further expression in the Charter of the Economic Rights and Duties of States which declared 'no state shall be compelled to grant preferential treatment to foreign investment,' (Chapter II, Article 2a), and 'transnational corporations shall not interfere in the internal affairs of a host State' (Article 2b).[11] The new approach sees the right of development as a positive benefit right – 'a ('have-not') member of the international community of states shall be entitled, when facing development problems and a shortage of resources, to corresponding assistance as a matter of an obligation on the part of ('have') members of the international economic community.'[12] The Secretary-General of the United Nations, on the other hand, claims a general consensus for a much broader conception of the right to development embracing:

(i) recognition that the realization of human potentialities in harmony with the community was the central purpose of development; consequently the human person must be seen as the subject and not the object of development as a process requiring the satisfaction of both material and non-material basic needs.

(ii) respect for the entire range of fundamental human rights specified in the International Bill of Human Rights[13] and for the principles of equality and non-discrimination as fundamental to the development process.

(iii) The achievement of a degree of individual and collective self-reliance must be an integral part of the development process – each individual must be able to participate fully in shaping his own reality.[14]

This approach led Theodoor Van Boven, the Director of the United Nations Division of Human Rights, to conclude that 'the right to development is a holistic concept which seeks to create a synthesis of a whole range of existing human rights which are informed and given an extra dimension by the emergence of a growing international consensus on a variety of development objectives.'[15] Karel de Vey Mestdagh endorses this approach but concludes from it that the 'right' to development is not a distinctive human right but only 'an aggregate of existing rights'. He suggests that the only way in which it makes sense to treat the right of development as a human right is as 'an instrumental right (or rather a right of an instrumental nature)' which 'assists in the more effective implementation of existing rights,' a means 'of exerting pressure on the international community to implement the right whose existence and substance are not in dispute'. What Mestdagh appears to have in mind by pressure, however, is only the general weight of world opinion that the richer states should come to the aid of the poorer. 'The bearer of the right is the impoverished state, the bearer of the obligation the state which is in a position to provide assistance.'[16] In these weak terms the right to development appears rather as an instrumental *principle* than an instrumental *right*; since not only is there no way of enforcing a right to assistance but it is not apparent how one could establish either the assistance which a poor state is entitled to receive or a rich state required to give.

The right to development is often claimed as one of the third generation of solidarity rights (the first generation being the traditional liberal-democratic civil and political rights and the second generation the economic, social and cultural rights), a group embracing the right to peace, the right to a healthy and ecologically-balanced environment and the right to enjoy the common heritage of mankind. The distinctive characteristic of all these rights is that they are essentially not rights that can be enjoyed by individuals as members of a particular community, and therefore claimable from each person's own state, but claims made on behalf of the peoples in particular states or in all states against both the Governments and the peoples of other states and of the international community of states. It is an open question as to whether it is possible to establish meaningful rights of this character. As far as the concept of the right to development itself is concerned I am inclined to the view that, while it is at present more in the nature of a principle than a right, according it the status of a right increases the likelihood that steps will be taken to secure implementation of the essential objectives which the principle embodies. It has to be recognized, however, that whereas the negative right of a state to non-interference by other states in its internal affairs may be held to be an unqualified right against each and every state, the right to assistance cannot be unqualified against any other state or against the community of states. Just as the benefit rights of individuals in a society are not an expression of each individual's own assessment of his needs, so the needs of poor societies cannot be self-established and asserted as rights against rich societies. Moreover the need deficiencies of a poor country may derive not only from a lack of resources, knowledge or skill, but from an absence of incentives, the existence of cultural values or institutions inhibiting development, serious internal conflict or instability, or a high degree of inefficiency or corruption within the economy or the Government service. These are all relevant factors not only to any assessment of needs, but to the ascription to or assumption by other states of an obligation to provide assistance. As Professor Wolff insisted at the 1981 Montreal International Law Association Conference 'The Right of Development is not an inalienable right it is an *earned right*.'[17] But 'earning a right' to development aid should not be a matter of satisfying the conditions specified by a potential donor, but rather of meeting the requirements of development specified by the Secretary-General as representing the general consensus of United Nations members: the satisfaction of the material and non-material needs of the individual persons of the community concerned; the achievement of individual and collective self-reliance and the realization of fundamental human rights, civil and political as well as economic and social.

The right of development should be treated not as an attractive but practically irrelevant piece of political window-dressing, but as a real opportunity for giving international effect to the objective put forward by the Norwegian Agency of International Development that 'Our development cooperation work must not strengthen the forces of political repression nor those which stand in the way of social justice . . . both political freedom and social justice must be developed to the full.'[18] The mode of implementation will need to provide encouragement for both rich and poor countries to enter into agreements which promote economic development as part of the broader human perspectives outlined by the United Nations Secretary-General. What is required is a general code of practice for all development agreements which all state authorities and all international agencies would bind themselves to give effect to. That skeleton code of practice would then need to be made flesh by spelling out specific commitments for the particular development and particular state concerned. It would be unrealistic to expect dramatic results from the implementation of proposals on these lines, but by requiring states seeking material aid to take steps to fulfil their subjects' non-material rights they might lead at least some states to recognize the practical truth that 'all human rights and fundamental freedoms are indivisible and interdependent.'[19]

RIGHTS OF CITIZENS – THE RIGHT TO VOTE

The concept of persons as bearers of liberty rights of protection and of non-interference against the state is incompatible with arbitrary or absolute rule. Individual rights require a framework of constitutional government upholding the rule of law, with legal rights and duties strictly defined and upheld by independent courts. The members of such a community are not mere passive subjects with duties of compliance and submission to the ruler's will, but active citizens with both rights and obligations to the society which they collectively constitute. The historical change from subject to citizen was a recognition that public affairs were not the exclusive prerogative of the Crown and Government but were of legitimate concern to members of the community at large. Implicit in the notion of citizenship, though only gradually accepted and realized in practice, is the claim of universality, since all are affected by the activities of Government and all contribute to the common weal through their respective labours. Citizen rights of participation in civic affairs are therefore rights to which all men, and later all women, were held entitled by virtue of being members of the community, irrespective of birth or status, wealth or position. Most civic rights appear as complements of liberty rights of non-interference by state authorities and are difficult to express other than in universal terms. How could one argue a claim to a right to petition the Government, to hold public meetings or to publish pamphlets or newspapers on behalf of only some members of the community? Restrictions of this character have to be made in terms of the requirements of the public order or public good and consequently need application to the citizenry in general. But what then of the right to vote?

It is important to stress at the outset that all political rights are instrumental rights, whose importance lies in the ends which the right concerned may be used to secure. Consequently arguments about the nature and requirements of political rights will, when used in debates about the desirability of restricting or extending political rights, be coloured by the expectations of the political consequences which will follow from the changes projected. This is particularly the case with the right to vote. From the seventeenth to the nineteenth century the great fear of the propertied classes in England was that an extension of the franchise to the poor would threaten their wealth and position. If the propertyless were given the vote 'why should not those men vote against all property?' argued General Ireton in the Commonwealth Army Debates at Putney in October 1647.[20] The seventeenth-century Levellers, like the Chartists two hundred years later, had no designs against the institution of property as such but they did indeed threaten to use the franchise they demanded to promote the interests of the poor and weak against the rich and powerful.

Though voting may be used for selection of particular office-holders or to decide particular issues, its main purpose has been to secure the election of representatives to the legislature. William Cobbett wrote 'The great right, therefore, of every man, the right of rights, is the right of having a share in the making of the laws, to which the good of the whole makes it his duty to submit.'[21] For Cobbett, as for his great radical predecessor Thomas Paine, there were no grounds for denying the right to vote to those who did not possess a certain amount of property. Since all men paid taxes, direct or indirect, and all men had an obligation to fight for their country and to uphold its laws, it followed that all had a right to elect those whose task it was to exact the taxes, frame the laws and embark on wars.[22] Further as it was impossible to show that the mere possession of property ensured its possessors of the qualities of moral probity or rational discernment conducive to the proper choice of representatives, a property qualification had the effect of guaranteeing the vote to idle, ignorant, corrupt men of property while denying it to industrious, enlightened, virtuous working men. The same damning charge could be made against rules granting the vote to men while denying it to women, or to all members of some race, colour, nationality or ethnic group, while denying it to all members of other groups.

There is a sense in which an age requirement for voting has a similarly arbitrary effect, excluding the otherwise well-qualified able under-age person in favour of the otherwise ill-qualified person of the required age. But the situation is, in fact, crucially different in that, whereas there is not only no need but no justification for excluding any persons on grounds of sex or race, there is both a clear need and justification for excluding all persons at *some* age. What one has to accept is that the age point chosen between the stage of childhood and the stage of young adulthood is bound to be somewhat arbitrary and will inevitably exclude many who on all other counts are the equals or superiors of those entitled to the franchise. There is, however, a kind of rough justice and equity in making the age of entitlement to vote the same as the age of liability for conscription into the armed forces. In a realm of citizens rather than subjects the existence of a duty at a certain age to risk one's life in defence of the community argues strongly for a reciprocal right to vote to choose those representatives who have the power to require that duty to be carried out, at a possible risk of life and limb.

The largest category of persons excluded from the franchise are those who are not nationals of the state concerned, it being accepted as part of the logic of the nation state that only those who are either born in the national territory or who are naturalized persons should be accorded the rights of citizens in the state. Aliens presently resident will retain their citizen rights in the states of which they are nationals, unless they are one of those unfortunates who fall into the category of stateless persons. It is, of course, open to any state to permit resident aliens to exercise citizen rights, as Britain does with resident citizens of the Republic of Ireland.

If unnaturalized aliens may be denied citizen rights, as they are not members of the civic community, convicted criminals are often seen as persons who by their own actions have demonstrated their hostility to the community and thereby forfeited their right to participate in making the laws they have violated. There is force in this argument, though it has to be recognized that under many political systems persons will be deliberately convicted of criminal acts which they have not committed or which they are morally entitled to commit in terms of the International Bill of Human Rights. It also needs to be made plain that convicted criminals ought not to be treated as men without civic rights. Indeed precisely because of incarceration the criminal stands in urgent need of rights of petition and communication with the outside world to complain about his punishment or treatment in prison. Providing these civic rights are recognized and effectively secured, however, there would seem to be no objection in principle to the right to vote being denied to convicted criminals serving a prison sentence. This is the position taken up by the European Court of Human Rights.[23]

If the argument for denying convicted criminals the right to vote derives from their wilful anti-social behaviour, that for denying it to persons of unsound mind derives from their lacking the capacity of rational determination and choice, opening up the possibility of their vote being manipulated by others. While there is substance in the underlying argument the practical implications give rise to very considerable difficulties. Mental incapacity or unsoundness of mind are matters of degree and of disagreement among medical authorities both as to nature and treatment. The modern trend is strongly in the direction of seeking to help the mentally handicapped to live their own lives within the community, rather than isolated in large institutions. Moreover, it is simply not true that all those who are institutionalized are incapable of making rational choices. Two criteria may be useful here. The first is that no inmate ought to be denied the vote if there are mental out-patients of roughly the same mental condition included on the electoral register. Secondly all those confined to mental institutions whom it is proposed to exclude from the register should be given the right to appeal against the ruling, where demonstration of the capacity to make a meaningful appeal would be strong presumptive evidence that the appeal should be granted.[24]

The view that a minimum level of understanding ought to be a necessary condition for being accorded the right to vote has led a succession of writers, of whom the most celebrated was the liberal theorist John Stuart Mill, to champion educational or literacy qualifications for the exercise of the franchise.[25] The question that has to be asked here is not whether it is desirable that voters should be literate, but whether it is justifiable to deprive illiterate citizens of the right to vote. The imposition of a literacy qualification for voting is morally unacceptable unless adequate facilities are provided to enable the illiterate to become literate easily and quickly and to ensure that all children grow up literate. Literacy tests would also need to be set at a low level and not applied discriminatorily as between persons of different races etc., as they were in the states of the Deep South of the USA after the Civil War. On the other hand, it has to be recognized that any officially sponsored literacy campaign, especially one directed to meeting a literacy qualification for voting, is very liable to be framed and utilized by the authorities to secure the political adherence of the would-be literate to the Government in power. Blatant indoctrination is only avoidable under conditions of some real degree of political competition.

But the crucial question which has to be faced is whether it is acceptable that those at present illiterate should be denied the vote, especially in those countries where there is the expectation that large numbers will remain illiterate over a long period. Certainly it cannot be assumed that those unable to read or write are incapable of making rational choices, or that they cannot communicate or be communicated with. Whereas in the Western liberal states the days of hectic campaigning and packed political meetings have been largely superseded by television electioneering, these traditional methods of drumming up support are still the stable diet of electioneering in the Third World. It is, in any case, doubtful whether literacy, in the sense of communication through electoral literature, has ever played as important a role in influencing voters as visual and oral communication. The experience of elections in India since independence, and especially since first the rejection of Indira Gandhi and subsequently her return to power, strongly suggests that the granting of the franchise to illiterates, even where they form a majority of the population, is compatible with political democracy and political stability. Given that those excluded by a literacy qualification not itself overtly discriminatory will be overwhelmingly the poor, the disadvantaged and the downtrodden there are strong grounds for not denying to the suffering a vehicle which they may use to improve their depressed condition. Granted there is the danger that the oppressive rich and powerful, especially in rural areas, may 'muster' the votes of their poor dependents, this is a reason for demanding that the government take steps to ensure genuinely free elections, not for denying the vote to the oppressed.

While there is no difficulty in ascertaining those who legally have the right to vote, it does not necessarily follow that all those legally entitled are permitted to do so. It is the clear duty of the state to ensure that all those entitled to vote, and only those entitled to vote, are permitted to go to the polls and to vote freely without threat of coercion or fear of molestation. Above all the state has an especially strict duty not to resort to such practices itself. But since the right to vote is not an individual piece of property to be used for personal gain or advantage but a civic right to be used for the common good, it is both legitimate and necessary for the state to take steps to ensure that votes are neither bought nor sold; especially since electoral bribery is a device commonly used by the rich to secure their own advantage at the expense of the public good.

Rather more complex issues arise when one considers the use of coercion or the threat of coercion against voters. It will be useful here to distinguish between being forced to go to vote and being forced to vote for a particular candidate. The latter clearly makes a mockery of the conception of elections as the free choice of representatives and each state authority is under an obligation to forbid and prevent such practices. The former, however, where it assumes the form of a legal requirement to vote, is not incompatible with the conception of electoral choice. Under the Australian electoral system, for example, each registered voter has a legal duty to exercise his civic right to vote for any candidate he chooses, where the penalty for failing to vote is a fine. Since the purpose of the fine is to encourage a high electoral turn-out, without in any way inhibiting electoral choice, there would seem to be no objection in principle to a compulsory voting system, providing the penalty for non-compliance is not too high and that provision is made for the exemption of those with conscientious objection to voting.

Both the Universal Declaration of Human Rights and ICPR refer to universal and *equal* suffrage, an equality which has traditionally been expressed in the slogan, 'one man, one vote'. Equality may be undermined in a number of ways. Thus, if constituencies are grossly unequal in size a vote in one constituency will carry much more weight than a vote in another, a device which may be used to ensure that legislative power remains firmly in the hands of one section of the electorate. The position will be greatly aggravated if electors are allocated to different electoral rolls according to some criterion such as race, colour or income, with a much higher proportion of voters per seat on one roll than on the other. What must be particularly guarded against is the deliberate 'rigging' of electoral boundaries in order to produce grossly disparate-sized constituencies to the advantage of the ruling party. Changes in electoral boundaries ought to be formulated by independent boundary commissions and be subject to public discussion. But ought one to go further and insist in this age of political parties that 'equal suffrage' requires each vote to count equally in determining the final composition of the legislature? This would involve the use of some form of Proportional Representation (PR). Whatever one may personally think about the arguments in favour of PR it is, in my view, impossible to show that they are sufficiently strong or of such a character as to substantiate the claim that the First Past the Post (FPP) system constitutes an infringement of the right to vote which ought not to be permitted in any state. This has certainly also been the view of the European Court of Human Rights with regard to the member states of the Council of Europe.[26] While it may reasonably be claimed that PR is fairer than FPP, in that almost any PR system will produce a truer reflection of electoral opinion in the legislature, this does not entitle one to overrule as irrelevant the claims of stability and acceptability made on behalf of FPP; still less to require every existing legislature not elected by PR to abandon its existing electoral practices as being in violation of the right to vote.

The right to vote is an instrumental right which may be used to realize a variety of purposes. Though it is a right of individuals, it cannot be used by individuals to secure their particular ends except as part of a collective process. Moreover the ends which the franchise is meant to serve are not primarily the particular interests of individual voters but their common interests as members of a political community. That is not to say that the use of the franchise by individuals to seek to realize their sectional interests, as senior citizens for example, is illicit, but that regard should be had to the interests of other members of the community. In particular the franchise cannot legitimately be used by voters to preserve franchise restrictions in order to ensure that the legislature operates on behalf of those privileged to vote. Historical experience strongly suggests that a restricted franchise works directly to the advantage of those possessing the franchise and that adequate attention by the legislature to the needs of the poor and underprivileged is unlikely to be given until at least a substantial proportion of them have the vote.

The right to vote, unlike the rights of assembly or expression, is a positive instrumental right which cannot be exercised at all in the absence of state authorization, since one cannot exercise the vote except in state-run elections.[27] More crucially it must be insisted that its instrumental use must be subject to the requirements of other fundamental human rights; thus it must not serve discriminatory purposes. In particular it must be insisted that the right by election of a majority to govern cannot be a right to govern without regard to the human rights of the minority. An election may serve to legitimize a Government but it cannot give any Government authority to violate the fundamental rights of any of its citizens or subjects.

Elections serve different purposes according to the nature of the political system in which they operate and the nature and extent of the freedom of choice which they provide to the voter. One may distinguish between two kinds of electoral choice – of constituency representatives and of the government. Since there are no instances of voters being allowed a free choice of the executive but not of the legislature we may classify elections into three categories:[28]

(i) competitive elections
   where voters choose both legislative representatives and the Government, either directly or indirectly;
(ii) semi-competitive elections
   where voters choose legislative representatives but not the Government, though the composition and policy of the Government is influenced by the outcome of the legislative elections;

(iii) non-competitive elections
where voters choose neither legislative representatives nor the Government.

The first category is that of the Western liberal democratic type of election, where the composition of both the legislature and the executive is not known or determined in advance but depends directly on the outcome of the individual choices made by millions of voters between candidates from a number of political parties. The third is the Communist-type election, where all candidates are members of the ruling party or of a satellite party, and where either no choice of candidates is permitted or where choice of candidates is permitted only in a minority of constituencies under conditions which strongly favour the Government-preferred candidate. In such states not only the political character of the Government but its specific composition and the composition of the legislature is decided in advance by the ruling party. Any changes in the composition of both bodies will reflect not the expressed intentions of the voters, since virtually no room for such expression exists, but the outcome of deliberations and struggles within the highest counsels of the governing party.

In between these two well-defined categories we have a large group of states which permit some degree of competition and choice, but where the form, nature and extent of the competitive choice varies markedly not only between states, but often between different parts of the same state. In this category we may distinguish four main types of semi-competitive election. Firstly there are the elections in one-party, non-monolithic states, like Kenya and Tanzania, where electors have a free choice between locally nominated party candidates resulting at times in the defeat of Ministers standing for re-election. Consequently, while the political nature of the Government is not at issue, the composition and to some degree the policies of the Government are; although the main concern of electors tends to be with local problems and personalities. Under this system both ordinary members of the Legislature and Government Ministers are likely to pay considerable heed to representations made by local bodies with regard to local issues.

The second form of semi-competitive election is to be found in those states where there exist a number of parties, each associated with a particular racial, tribal, national, ethnic or religious group, with each party effectively in control of some part of the country. Under these conditions most voters will both find themselves confronted by a candidate of only one party and most will identify with that party as the natural embodiment of the group to which they belong. In the mixed frontier areas between the groups and in the large cities of mixed composition the outcome of the election may well depend on the relative success of the different parties in getting out the 'ethnic' vote. While the great majority of voters will have no choice between candidates, and while the general political pattern the legislature will assume can be gauged in advance, the electoral outcome will be an assembly of competitive groups. Where one ethnic group has a built-in majority there is often no immediate prospect of its being able to secure an accommodation with opposition parties, nor any incentive for it to promote policies to attract opposition voters away from the parties of their natural allegiance. In time, however, this may change.

The third form of semi-competitive election is to be found in countries, like some Latin American states, where in the rural areas and in some urban slum areas one has clientalist voting with powerful patrons coercing or bribing voters subject to their control to vote *en bloc* for the party of the patron's choice and different patrons negotiating agreements with different party leaders. The result is that while the client voters have no electoral choice, the resulting assembly will consist of competing party groups with opposition parties being able to exercise varying degrees of influence on the Government.

The final type of semi-competitive election is to be found where we have a state-licensed party system designed to ensure that the Government always wins elections, while presenting both to the general populace and to outside Governments a semblance of Western-style electoral choice. 'Loyal opposition' parties are permitted to campaign, often relatively freely in the major cities, but are 'dissuaded' from venturing into Government strongholds where appropriate steps are taken to 'discourage' voters who might be otherwise inclined to choose to vote for opposition candidates. The opposition representatives elected from the minority of 'open' seats are expected to restrict their activities to limited criticism and to accept a permanent minority status.

In assessing which, if any, of these forms of semi-competitive election may be regarded as compatible with the right of every citizen 'to vote and to be elected at genuine periodic elections which shall be by universal and equal suffrage' to 'be held by secret ballot guaranteeing the free expression of the will of the electors' (ICPR,

Article 25(b)),[29] it is important to note the inherent characteristics of 'free expression of the will of the electors' under the Western liberal democratic system. In all Western states electors are conditioned by upbringing and by cultural ·environment to act electorally in accordance with the values and requirements of the established political system, and in particular to vote for existing parties identified with that system. Most Western voters thus see electoral choice in terms of a choice between constitutional democratic parties to determine which of them shall govern the country until the next election. The stability of such a system is dependent on the major competing parties being genuinely committed to the rules of constitutional political competition, such that each can contemplate the electoral victory of its opponents as no threat either to its existence or to its future ability to compete for office. It is not surprising that such conditions are not commonly found or readily secured in the majority of states in the world; especially in countries which are sharply divided along ethnic, racial, national or religious lines. If the conception of the right to vote as a realizable right of meaningful choice is to have any application outside the privileged, long-established societies of the Western world, it will be necessary to proceed on the basis of minimum 'realizable' rather than optimum 'desirable' requirements.

The core of any free expression of the right to vote must be some minimum degree of free choice, and choice cannot be exercised in the absence of alternatives. No electoral system is acceptable, therefore, which does not provide the possibility of electoral choice to voters. Where electors are faced with no choice of candidate this should result from the genuine unwillingness of other candidates to present themselves, not from action taken by state authorities or others to prevent or deter further candidates from standing. In this respect it is noteworthy that I CPR speaks of the right of every citizen 'to vote and to be elected' (Article 25b).[30] Individual candidatures running on a personal ticket are compatible with the maintenance of a one-party state and afford a channel through which voter dissatisfaction may be expressed. However, if voters are to have any real opportunity of exerting any influence in a one-party state it must be through the process for electing party candidates. This may be secured in one of two ways, either by allowing voters in each constituency a real and direct say in the selection of the party candidate, or by permitting several party candidates to be nominated for election.

A more extensive and meaningful choice is afforded in semi-competitive elections under multi-party conditions, especially where popular pressure can be exerted on the state authorities to require them to fulfil their responsibility to ensure that coercion and threats are not used against candidates wishing to stand for election. Where only approved parties are licensed or permitted to compete, electors and parties have the right to know the terms of and reasons for the restrictions in operation, restrictions which should in any event be subject to appeal to an independent judicial body. Licensed parties have a right to expect both that they will be permitted to put up as many candidates as they wish, and that they will be afforded state protection in their legitimate electoral activities.

There can be no justification for a governing party refusing, as a matter of principle, to permit other parties to contest elections; since it is precisely the permanent, unquestioned entitlement of the governing to govern unchecked which the right to vote exists to deny. If 'the will of the people' is to be 'the basis of the authority of Government,' as laid down in the United Nations Universal Declaration of Human Rights (Article 21.3),[31] it cannot rightfully rest with the Government concerned to determine how that will shall be expressed, still less to determine the outcome of its expression. A case may be made for autocratic paternalistic rule; but it cannot be made on the basis of a spurious Government assertion to act as the embodiment of a popular will when it is that Government's primary concern to prevent any will being manifested other than that it has itself manufactured or manipulated.

Free electoral choice also requires that both electors and nominated candidates shall have freedom of expression, to question candidates, criticize existing representatives and government policies, and to put forward proposals of their own, without interference from the Government and under the protection of the Government. Government authorities have a special responsibility to ensure that voting procedures and practices are fair and that announced results accurately reflect the expressed will of the electorate. The elected representatives themselves must be accorded full freedom of expression and criticism of the authorities. Since the proper role of the authorities in elections is to permit the free expression of the will of the electors they may legitimately take action against those seeking to prevent this; whether by the direct violation of the rights of electors or by the advocacy of discriminatory policies designed to deprive some sections of the community of their fundamental rights.

9
Problems of Implementation

'All human beings are born free and equal in dignity and rights. They are endowed with reason and conscience and should act towards one another in a spirit of brotherhood.'[1]

These opening words of the Universal Declaration of Human Rights express a conception of man which underpins the whole framework of human rights embodied in the Universal Declaration and the two International Covenants of Human Rights. It is a conception which, while it derives most directly from Western political traditions, is in harmony with moral and social teachings to be found in many other traditions and patterns of belief.[2] The overwhelming endorsement and subsequent reaffirmation of the Universal Declaration by the United Nations General Assembly afford striking evidence of the extraordinary status and appeal of its principles and precepts, compelling Governments of all forms and persuasions to publicly recognize their obligation to ensure that all persons within their jurisdiction are accorded the rights specified.

Thirty-five years have passed since the adoption of the United Nations Declaration of Human Rights, during which time agreement has been reached on a number of important Conventions and Declarations laying down standards for human rights observance and providing the international machinery to further their implementation. Yet gross and widespread violation of even the most elementary rights continues in states which are themselves party to these same Conventions and Declarations. Why should this be so? In one sense it is not surprising since there is no way in which an International body like the United Nations, based on the principles of 'the sovereign equality of all its Members' and non-intervention in matters 'essentially within the domestic jurisdiction of any State,' could require a member state to implement even those human rights obligations which it had voluntarily assumed.[3] Human rights implementation is, and must remain for the foreseeable future, a matter 'essentially within the domestic jurisdiction' of individual states. What has to be considered, therefore, is why states fail to provide domestic remedies for human rights infringements or failures.

While it might be argued that this question·cannot be discussed except in terms of specific rights within particular societies, each understood in terms of its own distinctive history, cultural values and beliefs, institutions and practices, it is necessary to insist on the overriding nature of fundamental human rights claims. Though the setting and form of a particular right may vary from one society to another, such variation may not be at the expense of the right concerned. In this final chapter I have, therefore, taken the most important rights discussed earlier and grouped them into the following categories according to the nature of the rights, and the issues raised in securing their implementation:

(i)   right to the rule of law;
(ii)   liberty rights to non-coercion;
(iii)   liberty rights to non-interference;
(iv)   political rights;
(v)   economic and social rights.

(i) Right to the rule of law
The concept of human rights as the rights which all men and women in all societies ought to have secured, protected and enforced under the law derives from and is dependent on the conception of society based on the rule of law. The right of the members of all states to be governed by law and not arbitrary fiat imposes on all Governments the strict, unqualified obligation to confine its activities to those specifically authorized by constitutionally enacted, publicly promulgated, legislation. Since the body most likely to be tempted to disregard formal legal restrictions is the Government, it is a cardinal necessity of the rule of law that there exist independent courts not subject to executive control to whose determination the Government, like all other bodies and persons, is subject. Whether the courts in any country are independent of the executive can readily be determined by seeing whether in cases of prosecution by the state of alleged political offenders the outcome is never in doubt, since it is precisely in such cases that Government influence is most likely to be exerted. Where

the politically accused are always found guilty and the only point at issue is the severity of the sentence, we may conclude that the judiciary is not independent. Where the courts are dependent on or subservient to the executive the whole conception of human rights as legal rights is undermined, since to have a legal right is to have a claim which one can have substantiated by an independent judicial ruling.

States where the judiciary is subverted by the executive must be distinguished from those where the state authorities fail to take steps to protect members of the judiciary from outside threats or pressures, or fail to remove judges guilty of gross partiality or corruption. Similarly, one must distinguish between those states where the police authorities are required, authorized or encouraged to act outside the law and those where the Government fails to take steps to forbid and punish such practices. In the former instances the Government is itself directly and deliberately responsible for the subversion of the rule of law: in the latter it has wilfully failed in its obligation to maintain the rule of law, though one has to recognize, however, that this obligation can never be fully and effectively discharged. No Government can eliminate police harassment and brutality or judicial bias and corruption, but all can legitimately be expected to take steps to prevent such practices.

An independent judiciary has no place or purpose except within a legal framework designed to secure a fair trial, as the embodiment of legal justice and as the inalienable right of the accused. Here again we may distinguish between the paramount duty of the state not itself to prevent fair trials and its obligation to take steps to ensure that the course of justice is not perverted by others. The former requires no more than self-restraint and non-interference and costs nothing; the latter requires positive action designed to prevent others interfering with the judicial process. The latter is much more difficult to secure than the former and can never be fully secured. Innocent men will occasionally be found guilty no matter how strict the legal safeguards. What one needs to determine in any state is whether the authorities fail to take elementary precautions to prevent interference with justice, or whether they acquiesce or even participate in the judicial process being suborned to serve the interests of the rich and powerful over the poor and weak.

In this connection it is encouraging to note the continued concern of jurists in Third World states, especially Commonwealth states, for the maintenance of the rule of law. One-party rule as practised in these states is not based on an ideological rejection of judicial independence, as in Communist states.[4] It is liable, however, to give rise to severe tensions between a judiciary committed to upholding individual rights under the law and a one-party state Government determined to realize its own, often self-interested, conception of the public interest, if necessary in spite of the law.

In moving from the area of rights constitutive of the concept of the rule of law to the wider domain of substantive human rights it is important to stress the guiding influence of the former concept. The notion of law as the individual citizen's protection against unauthorized or unwarranted interference, whether by other persons or the state itself, informs the whole area of human rights.

(ii) Liberty rights to non-coercion

> not to be killed or deprived of the means of life
> not to be subjected to torture or to inhuman punishment or treatment
> not to be forced to adopt or renounce a Faith
> not to be forced to marry
> not to be enslaved
> not to be subject to forced labour

The rights in this category are inherent in the concept of society as a community existing to protect its members from coercion. With the exception of the right not to be subject to forced labour, these are paramount rights which may never be infringed; although the right to life may be forfeit by a person legally convicted of a capital offence. Forced labour may never be imposed by a private person or body but, subject to its not involving inhuman treatment or being under inhuman conditions, it may be required of convicted prisoners or of ordinary members of the community in periods of war or of proclaimed emergencies. What is distinctive about the rights in this category is that their rigid enforcement can never involve any infringement of another person's fundamental rights. Nothing but good can flow from absolute observance of the rights of non-coercion and nothing but evil from their violation. While it will be necessary to legally define the coercive acts which may never be resorted to, and while differences of definition may exist in different legal codes, there is no room for dispute as to what constitutes the core of the right concerned. It is clear that certain forms of pain infliction, such as the extraction of finger nails, constitute torture and that such acts are always wrong.

The state has two obligations with respect to rights of non-coercion – not itself to commit violations and to act to prevent or punish violation by others. The first obligation raises no problems of authority or capacity – all that is required of a ruling power is the will to desist from committing violations. Far from resources being needed to enforce rights to non-coercion, resources will be released for more positive purposes as violating states wind down the apparatus of state repression. Where rights violations directly stem from Government policy decisions the more effective the Government apparatus the greater the degree of violation. Better an ineffective tyranny than an effective one. The reverse is true with respect to violations carried out by others in spite of the state, since this requires harnessing a will to suppress violations to the effective deployment of adequate resources. While no Government is in a position to prevent some violation of the paramount rights of non-coercion, the extent of the infringements will turn directly on the capacity of the authorities to act. In most cases it should be possible for state authorities to win the support of the bulk of the population and to overcome, or at least contain, those threatening life and security; but in some societies, as in the Lebanon or Northern Ireland, the divisions may be so wide and deep as to present no prospect of resolution.

Where the state authorities are directly responsible for widespread violation of the paramount rights of non-coercion their only response to public criticism or protest is likely to be increased repression. In such circumstances the problem is not one of justifying acts of rebellion but of carrying them out successfully.[5] Where the rights violations are on such a scale and of such a character as to constitute genocide the United Nations Convention of 1948 recognizes that intervention may be justified to prevent or suppress such acts and to punish those responsible 'whether they are constitutionally responsible rulers, public officials or private officials'. The Convention also provides for disputes between contracting parties relating to the responsibility of the state for genocide to be submitted to the International Court of Justice 'at the request of any of the parties to the dispute'.[6] It has to be recognized, however, that the International Court of Justice lacks any enforcement powers, and that the United Nations would be unlikely to be able or willing to contemplate intervention, unless the violating party were weak and the major powers united in opposition to it.

(iii) Liberty rights to non-interference

freedom to marry and have children
freedom of belief
freedom of movement
freedom of expression, association and assembly

What this group of rights have in common is that they are all claims to recognition of the right of individuals not to be interfered with in areas of life crucial to personal self-determination and development. Liberty rights to non-interference, unlike liberty rights to non-coercion, cannot be absolute, unqualified rights; since unlike the latter, which seek absolute protection from specific, evident evils, the former seek to protect certain important areas of free activity from outside interference irrespective of the purpose of the activity or of the interference. But it is not possible to claim that all interference with freedom in these areas must be wrong, no matter what the form of the activity undertaken or the purpose the intervention is designed to serve. Instead of being faced with the issue of how the universally recognizable core of a right to non-coercion may legitimately be defined under different legal systems, we have the quite different question of substantiating what the core area of each non-interference right should be. Some degree of restriction will be required for each liberty right to non-interference in order to protect legitimate rights of other parties, while other restrictions may be justifiable having regard to the values and traditions of particular societies. In Chapters 3 and 4 I have sought to establish with respect to each liberty right what is the minimum area of freedom which must not be infringed if there is to be freedom of choice and activity. What remains to be done is to appraise the barriers which stand in the way of securing these core areas in different societies with differing political systems. Such an appraisal would also provide an opportunity to reconsider the precise form and extent of the core areas of each right requiring protection.[7]

Whereas with paramount rights to non-coercion there appears to be an overwhelming case for requiring immediate implementation by all states, with rights to non-interference there appear to be valid reasons for adopting a more flexible approach which takes account of the varying social norms, values and life-styles to be found in different societies. The appropriate aim here would be to secure the progressive realization of the areas of non-interference rights and to judge individual societies according to whether the policies they pursue foster or inhibit such realization.

Particular problems arise with rights to freedom of expression, association and assembly which are regarded by most Governments with some degree of suspicion or hostility, but which are vital both in themselves and as means for securing and protecting other human rights. While the progressive realization of these rights must have regard to the legitimate responsibilities of Governments, especially in societies riven with social conflict and instability, it cannot be accepted that Governments are entitled to impose such restrictions as they think fit. The grounds and purposes of all limitations need to be publicly established and provision made for the gradual removal of those restrictions which seriously inhibit their exercise.

The rights of freedom of expression, association and assembly are vital ingredients of the rights of citizens to which we must now turn.

(iv) Political rights

> to organize and join political parties and associations
> to criticize Government policies and leaders
> to vote in free elections to choose both legislative representatives and the Government

The right of all citizens 'to take part in the conduct of public affairs, directly or through freely chosen representatives,' (ICPR, Article 25 (a)),[13] if it is to be meaningful, requires the specific citizen rights set out above. A Government can only be made responsible to the Governed if the former is removable by the latter. Under present-day conditions this means that citizens require the right to vote out the Government of the ruling party in free elections and to replace it by a Government of a different party. But to put forward a human rights demand in these terms is to assert that all the Communist States and all the one-party states of the Third World lack any legitimate political authority and need to transform the political and constitutional foundations of their political systems accordingly. It is unrealistic, however, to expect the present political leaders of these states, as both beneficiaries of and commonly believers in the existing order, to carry through such transformations, especially since the outcome in many cases would be their own political eclipse. Moreover, given the condition of instability and divisiveness existing in many of the Third

World states, any legalization of alternative political parties might well result in a high level of instability deriving from conflict between parties organized on a tribal or ethnic basis.

It, therefore, seems more realistic and more positive to lay stress on the right of citizens to participate in politics in ways which do not directly threaten the existence of one-party states. The 1976 *International Seminar on Human Rights, Their Protection and the Rule of Law in One-Party States* claimed that there was no necessary reason why one-party states should restrict freedom of expression and freedom of association except as 'the right to associate in alternative political parties or openly to advocate a revision to multi-party forms. Members . . . were agreed that it was vital to keep the one-party system alive through constructive criticism and comment and to preserve the right to associate in all groups other than those with an overtly political base.'[9] On this basis political participation might be acceptable to and supportive of a one-party regime while providing real outlet for the expression of grievances and criticism of the Government and its policies.

In the area of human rights the most urgent and pertinent of citizens' rights is the right to form associations devoted to the realization of the human rights embodied in the United Nations Universal Declarations and the two International Covenants. No Government, and particularly no State Party to the Covenants, has any right to prevent its citizens campaigning for the implementation of these rights or drawing attention to the infringement of rights, whether by the state or other bodies. Both International Covenants, indeed, in their respective preambles proclaim that 'the individual, having duties to other individuals and to the community to which he belongs, is under a responsibility to strive for the promotion and observance of the rights recognized in the present Covenant.'[10] Human rights are violated in all states of the world but, not surprisingly, the violations are most widespread and severe in those countries where no human rights associations are permitted to exist legally and to operate publicly.

In human survival terms the most urgent and compelling of the rights of citizens is the right in every state to form associa ions to campaign for peace and for changes in the defence policies and activities of their own Government, especially where such Governments possess or are planning to possess nuclear weapons.[11] The refusal of the Soviet Union to permit independent peace activity within its borders or within the Eastern bloc is a major factor inhibiting the effectiveness of peace movements in the West. Meanwhile the two great nuclear powers roll the globe down the path to thermo-nuclear oblivion in fruitless pursuit of security through nuclear superiority.

(v) Economic and social rights

to form and join trade unions
to work or maintenance
to just and favourable conditions of work
to an adequate standard of living
to social security, assistance and welfare
to health
to education

It is important to stress at the outset that the conception of economic and social rights requires to be underpinned by the constitutive rights inherent in the concept of a legal system based on the rule of law. For economic and social *rights*, as distinct from discretionary benefits, to exist individuals must be able to seek redress from independent courts against the failure of state authorities to provide the rights guaranteed by law or to prevent others interfering with their provision. Further, the concept of human rights as universal rights requires that neither the law nor its application permits discrimination in rights provision, except insofar as positive discrimination can be justified in terms of special need.

Where the law fails to provide the economic and social rights to which all men and women are entitled it must be open to those denied such rights to campaign for their realization, making use of the rights of freedom of expression, assembly and association, particularly association in free trade unions. Economic and social rights are essentially the rights of the poor and weak, rather than the rights of all. The rich and powerful in poor and weak states are able to secure levels of living and service commensurate with their opposite numbers in the rich and powerful states. But whereas in the latter states those in need have substantiable and realizable benefit rights claims against their own society and Government, the overwhelming mass who constitute the needy in the Third World cannot have their legitimate claims satisfied, since their societies lack adequate resources. What the poor and weak in such societies do have a legitimate and substantiable right to is not to be ill-treated and grossly exploited by the rich and powerful, and the right to expect, and where necessary require, their Governments to act in support of the exploited, not the exploiters.

It cannot be gainsaid, however, that to secure the progressive realization of economic and social rights at anything other than a snail's pace will for the great majority of the Third World population require substantial assistance from the more fortunate peoples of the Western and Communist worlds. While there is no way in which assistance could conceivably be demanded as a legal entitlement from such states and enforced through an international court, there is no inherent reason why, given the will and the understanding, the richer nations should not bind themselves to securing the progressive realization of economic and social rights in the Third World under terms and conditions designed to ensure that the assistance directly benefits those in need and encourages initiative and self-reliance, rather than passivity and dependence. But that will and understanding is all too lamentably lacking at present in both the Western and the Communist states, particularly in the USA and the USSR.

There is today a growing recognition that the most fundamental of man's requirements and claims cannot be met within the existing framework of sovereign nation states. If mankind is to survive the threat of nuclear war, and the less obvious but hardly less urgent threat presented by the gradual breakdown in the ecological balance of nature, drastic action is required. But because of the very nature of these threats no state is in a position to remove the dangers or to protect its citizens from their consequences. For the peoples of the Third World there is, as we have seen, a third and even more immediately real and painful threat to their survival presented by hunger, poverty and disease; calamities which it is quite beyond the capacities of their own states to avert. These survival rights of mankind are perhaps the most truly human rights, in that they are moral rights of all human beings against all human beings and against all political authorities, national and international; whereas other human rights are essentially moral rights of nationals against their fellow nationals and their own national state. The bitter dilemma presented by survival rights is that their urgent realization would require the most powerful nation states to drastically modify national policies of crucial concern to their political leaders and to submit to extensive and rigorous international inspection. Not only is there no way in which major states can be made to submit to international authority, but any authority established would be bound to be a compromise between the different positions taken up by the major state parties. In particular past experience shows that no agreement could be made unless it either excluded any effective enforcement powers, or made specific provision for them in an optional protocol binding only on those who separately sign their adherence.

The prospects then are bleak, but not without all hope. The very size and nature of the mounting catastrophe, especially nuclear catastrophe, may yet act as a spur to opposing state parties to make mutual concessions and submit to international authority rather than risk mutual obliteration and the eclipse of human life as we know it.[12]

Notes

PREFACE

1. *Amnesty International Report 1983* (Amnesty International Publications, 1983) p.1.

CHAPTER 1

1. Maurice Cranston, *What are Human Rights?* (The Bodley Head, 1973), p.21.
2. Professor A.J.M. Milne, 'The Idea of human rights: a critical enquiry', in *Human Rights' Problems, Perspectives and Texts*, edited by F.E. Dowrick (Saxon House, 1979), p.33.
3. Ibid., pp.29-36.
4. Richard Tuck, *Natural Rights Theories: Their origin and development*, (Cambridge University Press, 1979), especially Ch.7, 'The Radical Theory'.
5. The Putney Debates at the General Council of the Army, 28 October 1647, from the Clarke Manuscripts in *Puritanism and Liberty*, selected and edited by A.S.P. Woodhouse (J.M. Dent & Sons, 1938), p.53.
6. Universal Declaration of Human Rights (Article 2), in Ian Brownlie *Basic Documents on Human Rights* (2nd Edition), (Clarendon Press, Oxford, 1981), p.22.
7. Raymond Plant, 'The moral basis of welfare provision', Ch.4 in Raymond Plant, Harry Lesser and Peter Taylor-Gooby, *Political Philosophy and Social Welfare* (Routledge & Kegan Paul, 1980), pp.76-8.
8. In the reign of Elizabeth I men and women had no right to refuse to attend the services of the Established Church. Wrong believers (Catholics and Presbyterians alike), and non-believers who failed to do so, were subject to progressive fines, which could be ruinous.
9. See Preamble to the 'Universal Declaration of Human Rights', Brownlie, *Basic Documents on Human Rights*, pp.21-2.
10. Cranston, *What are Human Rights?*, pp.67-9.

11.   Though the main lines of arguments are drawn directly from Professor
       Ronald Dworkin I have strengthened and, in minor detail, amended
       them to meet my own requirements. Readers are referred to the original
       article, 'Taking Rights Seriously', in *Taking Rights Seriously* (Duckworth,
       1977), pp.184-205.
12.   Cranston, *What are Human Rights?* pp.67-8.
13.   Ibid., p.67.
14.   Plant is concerned by the absence of direct individual moral responsibility
       for ensuring the provision and fulfilment of welfare rights, which he sees
       as undermining the basis of the right to welfare he is seeking to establish.
       His solution is to place on individuals a strict moral obligation, not to
       meet the needs of deprived persons themselves, but to ensure that such
       needs are met. This responsibility would appear to involve (i) using one's
       influence and power (especially voting power) to ensure that the
       Government accepts and fulfils the obligations of society towards its
       needy members, and (ii) willingly doing what is required (e.g. paying
       one's taxes) to enable the Government to meet these obligations. (Plant,
       Political Philosophy and Social Welfare, pp.80-82). Such a conception
       might readily be applied to obligations to the needy in other countries as
       well as one's own.
15.   Cranston, *What are Human Rights?*, p.66.
16.   The European Coal and Steel Community has remained restricted to its
       original 1951 membership of France, West Germany, Italy, Belgium,
       Holland and Luxembourg.
17.   T.C. Hartley, *The Foundations of European Community Law*, (Clarendon
       Press, Oxford, 1981), Ch.10, 'Enforcement Actions', p.323.
18.   M.H. Mendelson points, however, to the increasing role played by the
       Court of Justice in this article, 'The European Court of Justice & Human
       Rights', *The Yearbook of European Law, I, 1981*, edited by F.G. Jacobs
       (Clarendon Press, Oxford, 1982).
19.   Currently all twenty-one members of the Council of Europe have signed
       the European Convention and all but Liechtenstein have ratified it.
20.   France refused to comply with a 1979 European Court ruling against her
       imposing import bans and a surcharge on Community 'sheepmeat',
       directed against British imports, and instead used its default as a weapon
       to secure British agreement to a Community scheme for mutton and
       lamb designed to protect French farmers.
21.   It is interesting to note that the Resolution of the Lagos Conference on
       the Rule of Law, 1961, sponsored by the International Commission of
       Jurists, '*Recognizes* that the Rule of Law is a dynamic concept which
       should be employed to safeguard and advance the will of the people and
       the political rights of the individual and to establish social, economic,
       educational and cultural conditions under which the individual may

achieve his dignity and realize his legitimate aspirations in all countries, whether dependent or independent.' Brownlie, *Basic Documents on Human Rights*, p.426.

22. Under the European Convention on Human Rights (Article 15i) 'In time of war or other public emergency threatening the life of the nation any High Contracting Party may take measures derogating from its obligations under this Convention to the extent strictly required by the exigencies of the situation, provided that such measures are not inconsistent with its other obligations under international law.' Under Article 15.3 the Party concerned is required to inform the Council of Europe of the measures it has taken and 'the reasons therefore'. In the case of the Greek Government's declaration on 21 April 1967 of a public emergency threatening the life of the Greek Nation, the European Human Rights Commission was not satisfied that the situation was in fact one of public emergency. It further found that even if it were accepted that an emergency existed, the measures taken went further than the situation required. See Francis G. Jacobs, *The European Convention on Human Rights* (Clarendon Press, Oxford, 1975), pp.206-7.

23. Fitzroy MacLean who attended the Moscow show trial in March 1938 of Bukharin, Rykov and others, records that Kretinski, a former Vice-Commissar for Foreign Affairs, when asked to account for his refusal to make the admissions of the guilt he had confessed to at the private preliminary hearing, replied '"I was forced to make them. Besides I know that if I said then what I say now, my statement would never reach the Heads of the Party and of the Government."' Next day Kretinski retracted and admitted his guilt in Court. *Eastern Approaches* (Jonathan Cape, 1949; Reprint Society, 1951), p.63.

24. See the United Nations *Declaration of the Protection of All Persons from being Subjected to Torture and Other Cruel, Inhuman or Degrading Treatment or Punishment*, (1975). Brownlie, *Basic Documents on Human Rights*, pp.35-37.

25. Ibid., pp.21-2.

CHAPTER 2

1. In terms of this argument, if it could be shown that other creatures or living things were self-conscious, sentient, creative beings in some sense or form, then a basis would exist for a claim to be made of the right of each one of them *individually* to be entitled to live.

2. Article 6 of the United Nations International Covenant on Civil and Political Rights (1966) states 'Every human being has an inherent right

to life. The right should be protected by law. No one shall be arbitrarily deprived of his life.' Brownlie, *Basic Documents on Human Rights*, p.130.

3. No man is, of course, under an obligation to exercise his right of self-defence, and in terms of strict pacifist moral principles believers will be under a moral obligation not to do so.

4. George P. Fletcher in his article 'The Right to Life', *Georgia Law Review*, Vol.13, No.14, Summer 1979, makes a useful distinction between justified killings as *infringements* of the right to life, and unjustified and intentional killings as *violations* of the right to life.

5. It might be argued that one who attacks another expects him to retaliate and accepts that risk. Indeed assailants may not only claim for themselves a right of defence if they are attacked, but regard defence against attackers as a right of all who are attacked.

6. R.M. Hare, *Moral Thinking: Its Levels, Method and Point* (Clarendon Press, Oxford, 1981), p.225.

7. The general question of guilt and innocence is discussed in Chapter 6.

8. An interesting discussion of capital punishment and other 'issues of life' discussed in this chapter is to be found in Jonathan Glover, *Causing Death and Saving Lives* (Pelican Books, 1977).

9. *On Human Life: Encyclical Letter of Pope Paul VI 'Humanae Vitae'*, (Catholic Truth Society, London, 1968), p.17.

10. *Contraception and Chastity*, by G.E.M. Anscombe (Catholic Truth Society, 1979).

11. In *Humanae Vitae* Pope Paul VI speaks to 'Rulers of Nations' as follows: 'Do not ever allow the morals of your Peoples to be undermined. Do not tolerate any legislation which would introduce into the family practices which are opposed to the natural and divine law – for the family is the primary unit in the state.' (p.22).

12. The Catholic Church accepts that where the death of the unborn child is an unintended, though foreseen, side effect of treatment necessary to save a mother's life (as with cancer of the uterus) such treatment is morally justifiable. *Abortion and the Right to Live: A joint statement of the Catholic Archbishops of Great Britain*, 24 January 1980 (Catholic Truth Society, London).

13. Roger Wertheimer, 'Understanding the Abortion Argument', in *The Rights and Wrongs of Abortion, a Philosophy and Public Affairs Reader*, edited by Marshall Cohen, Thomas Nagel and Thomas Scanlon (Princeton University Press, 1974).

14. The European Commission on Human Rights in *X v. UK*, 13 May 1980, held that 'if Article 2 were held to cover the foetus and its protection under this Article were, in the absence of any express limitation, seen as absolute, an abortion would have to be considered as prohibited even where the continuance of the pregnancy would involve a serious risk to

the life of the pregnant woman. This would mean that the 'unborn life' of the foetus would be regarded as being of higher value than the life of the pregnant woman. . . . The Commission finds that such an interpretation would be contrary to the object and purposes of the Convention.' *European Commission of Human Rights Decisions and Reports*, Vol. 19 (Strasbourg, 1980).

15. Michael Tooley mounts an attack on the 'potentiality principle' in his article 'Abortion and Infanticide', in *The Rights and Wrongs of Abortion*, by arguing that one needs to add a self-consciousness requirement before one can establish a right to life. I do not find his arguments persuasive.

16. Under English Law the father of the foetus, whether married to the mother or not, has no right to prevent the mother having an abortion or to be consulted about a proposed abortion, providing that the provisions of the Abortion Act 1967 are complied with.

17. See articles in section on 'Birth Defects' in *Moral Problems in Medicine*, edited with introductions by Samuel Gorovitz *et. al.*, (Prentice-Hall, New Jersey, USA, 1976), especially 'Editor's Introduction', pp.341-2, and Eliot Slater, 'Health Service or Sickness Service', p.352-3.

18. John M. Freeman, 'Is There a Right to Die – Quickly?', reprinted from *The Journal of Paediatrics*, 1972, in *Moral Problems in Medicine*, pp.355-6.

19. Quoted by Glover, *Causing Death and Saving Lives*, p.152.

20. See Richard M. Hare, 'Survival of the Weakest', in *Moral Problems in Medicine*.

21. The poignant issue of the age of death understanding is discussed in the extract from 'The Adolescent Patient's Decision to Die', by J.E. Schowalter, J.D. Ferholt and N.M. Mann, *Pediatrics*, 1973, published in *Moral Problems in Medicine*.

22. English Law does not impose on individuals a general obligation to save the lives of others, even where no danger would be incurred, as with a child drowning in three feet of water. Since, however, the public authorities cannot be expected to be on the spot to deal with such life-crisis situations there are strong grounds for asserting that the law should impose a duty on individuals to come to the aid of those whose life is in danger.

23. Brownlie, *Basic Documents on Human Rights*, p.122.

24. The United Nations Convention Relating to the Status of Refugees (1951 as amended by the 1966 Protocol) lays down that contracting states (eighty have become parties to the Convention) shall not impose penalties on account of illegal entry on refugees coming directly from a territory where their life or freedom was threatened, nor be expelled save on grounds of national security or public order (Articles 31 and 32). Article 1 states that the term refugee shall apply to persons who 'owing to well founded fear of being persecuted for reasons of race, religion, nationality,

membership of a particular social group or political opinion' are outside their own country and are unable or, owing to such fear, are unwilling to return to it. Brownlie, ibid., pp. 51 and 61-2.

25.   Article II of the Convention defines genocide as 'any of the following acts committed with intent to destroy, in whole or in part, a national, ethnic, racial or religious group, as such:

> (a) killing members of the group;
> (b) causing serious bodily or mental harm to members of the group;
> (c) deliberately inflicting on the group conditions of life calculated to bring about its physical destruction in whole or in part;
> (d) imposing measures intended to prevent births within the group;
> (e) forceably transferring children of the group to another group.

The Covenant is unique in explicitly recognizing that the state authorities may themselves be the instigators of genocide and in calling for the punishment of all those committing genocide 'whether they are constitutionally responsible rulers, public officials or private individuals'. (Article IV), Brownlie, ibid., pp.31-2.

26.   *The Brandt Report* recommends that 'The flow of official development finance should be enlarged by:

> 1. An international system of universal revenue mobilization, based on a sliding scale related to national income, in which East European and developing countries – except the poorest countries — would participate.
> 2. The adoption of timetables to increase Official Development Assistance from industrialized nations to the level of 0.7 per cent of GNP by 1985, and to 1 per cent by the end of the century.
> 3. Introduction of automatic revenue transfers through international levies on some of the following: international travel, the global commons, especially sea-bed minerals.' *North-South: A Programme for Survival. Report of the Independent Commission on International Development Issues.* Pan Books (London, 1980), pp.290-91.

27.   The American Declaration of the Rights and Duties of Man, adopted by the Ninth International Conference of American States in 1948, provides 'It is the duty of every able-bodied person to render whatever civil and military service his country may require for its defense and preservation, and, in case of public disorder, to render such service as may be in his power' (Article XXXIV). Brownlie, *Basic Documents on Human Rights*, p.386.

28.   It might be thought possible to secure an addition to Article 6 of ICCPR absolving the citizens of a state condemned by the United Nations as an

aggressor from any obligation to fight for his or her country but, since such an addition would require an Optional Protocol for which it would be difficult to get General Assembly approval and, since it would be open to any state party to ICCPR not to adhere to the Protocol, it is doubtful whether this is a very fruitful and practical line of approach.

29.　See Guenter Lewy, 'Superior Orders, Nuclear Warfare and the Dictates of Conscience', *American Political Science Review*, Vol. LV, No. 1, March 1961.

30.　There is no reference to a right of conscientious military objection in ICCPR, nor is it specifically required under the European Convention on Human Rights which, however, provides under Article 4.3(a) that the prohibition of forced labour shall not include 'any service of a military character or, in the case of conscientious objectors in countries where they are recognized, service exacted instead of compulsory military service.' Brownlie, *Basic Documents on Human Rights*, p.244.

31.　See Adam Roberts and Richard Guelff, *Documents On the Laws of War*, (Clarendon Press, Oxford, 1982), in particular 'The Geneva Convention Relative to the Protection of Civilian Persons in Time of War', 1949. The four 1949 Geneva Conventions have been endorsed by over 150 states.

32.　Brownlie, *Basic Documents on Human Rights*, p.3.

33.　Printed in Myres S. McDougall and W. Michael Reisman, *International Law in Contemporary Perspective – The Public Order of the World: Cases and Materials* (The Foundation Press, New York, 1981), p.1008.

34.　The USA and UK in signing the 1977 Geneva Protocol on the Protection of Victims of International Armed Conflicts each stated their understanding that the rules established were 'not intended to have any effect on and do not regulate or prohibit the use of nuclear weapons'. Roberts and Guelff, *Documents on the Laws of War*, p.462.

35.　Glover, *Causing Death and Saving Lives*, p.262.

CHAPTER 3

1.　On the second point see Ronald Dworkin 'What Rights Do We Have?', in his *Taking Rights Seriously* (Duckworth, 1977).

2.　H.L.A. Hart, 'Are There Any Natural Rights?', *Philosophical Review*, Vol. 64, (1955) reprinted in *Political Philosophy*, edited by Anthony Quinton, 'Oxford Readings in Philosophy', (Oxford University Press, 1967).

3.　'Specifically' in this context means covered by a specific law or valid legal ruling rather than specifically mentioned in a law or ruling.

4.　William L. Westermann, *The Slave Systems of Greek and Roman Antiquity* (The American Philosophical Society, Philadelphia, U.S.A., 1935), p.20.

5. William L. Westermann, 'Slavery and the Elements of Freedom in Ancient Greece'. *Quarterly Bulletin of the Polish Institute of Arts and Sciences in America*, January 1943, reprinted in M.I. Finley (ed.), *Slavery in Classical Antiquity: Views and Controversies* (W. Heffer & Sons, Cambridge, 1960), pp.26-7.

6. M.I. Finley, 'Was Greek Civilisation Based on Slave Labour?', *Historia* 8 (1959), reprinted in *Slavery in Classical Antiquity*, p.60.

7. The common view, in which Plato and Aristotle concurred, was that Greeks should not be enslaved by Greeks; but many were. Indeed Westermann notes that the Delphic manumissions record instances of the freeing of slaves who were fellow subjects and fellow residents of the same *polis* as their masters, *The Slave Systems of Greek and Roman Antiquity*, pp.44-5.

8. *Anti-Slavery Report, Series VII, Vol. 13, No. 1, December 1981*, The Anti-Slavery Society for the Protection of Human Rights, London, pp.15-20.

9. Marc Bloch, *Feudal Society*, translated by L.A. Manyon, (Routledge & Kegan Paul, 1961), Ch. XIX, 'Servitude & Freedom'.

10. At the end of the sixteenth-century the *Kabala* peasant became virtually a slave in law since state decrees removed from him the right to pay off his debt, or have someone else pay it off for him. His condition of debt-servitude thus became legally permanent. Jerome Blum, *Lord and Peasant in Russia From the Ninth to the Nineteenth Century* (Princeton University Press, New Jersey, 1961), p.94, contrasts 'black peasants' who decided to quit their lands and become landlords' peasants because they expected to benefit thereby, with those who were unable, through invasions, civil wars, pestilence, fire or famine to continue as independent cultivators, pp.245-6.

11. See Sven Lindquist, *Land and Power in South America*, translated by Paul Britten Austin (Penguin Books, 1979), pp.163-4.

12. Brownlie, *Basic Documents on Human Rights*, pp.44-9. See also Judith Ennew, *Debt Bondage: A Survey*, (Anti-Slavery Society Human Rights Series, Report No. 4, 1981).

13. 'Forced Labour in Humera', *Anti-Slavery Reports, Series VII, December 1981*, pp.20-25.

14. See Brownlie, *Basic Documents on Human Rights* p.177. Also ICCPR Article 83, ibid., p.131.

15. Quoted in Kurt Glaser & Stefan T. Possony, *Victims of Politics: The State of Human Rights* (Columbia University Press, New York, 1979), p.464. The dreadful world of Soviet-labour camps was revealed to the world in Solzhenitsyn's *Gulag Archipelago*.

16. See Francis G. Jacobs, *The European Convention on Human Rights*, pp.55-6.

17. The first form of vagrancy is that of 'able-bodied persons who, instead of working for their livelihood, exploit charity as professional beggars', or of 'persons who through idleness, drunkenness or immorality live in a state of vagrancy'. The second comprises 'persons found begging or picked up as vagrants,' when none of the circumstances specified in the first form apply. Judgement of the European Court of Human Rights, De Wilde, Ooms and Versyp Cases ('Vagrancy Cases'), 18 June 1971 (Strasbourg), pp.9-10.

18. In so far as begging does not assume a persistent or threatening form, there is no evident reason why it should be legally proscribed. Moreover in general terms a high level of begging in a society is indicative of a high level of abject poverty (as in India).

19. Nicholas Bethell records in the concluding pages of *The Last Secret: Forcible Repatriation to Russia, 1944-7* that in May 1952 Sir Anthony Eden, 'the architect of forcible repatriation in 1944', reporting to the House of Commons on the negotiations for peace in the Korean War between the United Nations and the Chinese and North Koreans, stated '"I am sure the House will feel that the United Nations Command has had no alternative but to resist the forcible repatriation of Communist prisoners-of-war who have shown such a strong determination to remain in the free world. I will not dwell on the practical difficulties of forcibly repatriating more than 62,000 men, many of whom could be expected to commit suicide on the way. It would, I think, clearly be repugnant to the sense of values of the free world to send these men home by force"'. p.211.

20. Lawrence Stone, *The Family, Sex and Marriage in England, 1500-1800*, Weidenfeld & Nicholson (1977), records that in the early sixteenth century it was alleged that Sir Edward Coke, ex-Chief Justice of England, abducted his daughter by force from her mother, tied her to a bed post and severely whipped her to force her to consent to a marriage with the mentally unstable brother of the Duke of Buckingham, with a view to restoring Sir Edward's lost favour at the Court. (p.183).

21. Quoted, *The Family, Sex and Marriage in England, 1500-1800*, pp.240-41.

22. Under the United Nations Supplementary Convention on the Abolition of Slavery, the Slave Trade, and Institutions and Practices Similar to Slavery, 1956, state parties undertake to abolish any institution or practice whereby 'the husband of a woman, his family, or his clan, has the right to transfer her to another person for value received or otherwise' or 'a woman on the death of her husband is liable to be inherited by another man'. Brownlie, *Basic Documents on Human Rights*, p.45.

23. Abdul Aziz Said, 'Human Rights in Islamic Perspective' in *Human Rights: Cultural and Ideological Perspectives*, edited by A. Pollis and P. Schwab (Praeger Publishers, New York, 1980), pp.91-3.

24. See for example Sultan Hussein Tabandeh, *A Muslim Commentary on*

the Universal Declaration of Human Rights, translated by F.J. Goulding, (F.T. Goulding, London, 1970) who writes on divorce 'Another reason why women should not be granted the right is that the generality of them are more gullible and credulous. Sexual desire may make a woman easy prey to the blandishments of salacious individuals who trap her into divorcing her husband merely to fulfil their own lusts. . . . A man is not so easily fooled nor lightly trapped into precipitate action by lustful feelings or sexual tactics.'

25.   See Michael and Ann Craft, *Sex and the Mentally Handicapped*, Institute of Marital Studies, The Tavistock Institute of Human Relations, 1975 (Gerald Duckworth & Co. 1970).

26.   Brownlie, *Basic Documents on Human Rights*, p.121.

CHAPTER 4

1.   Sultan Hussein Tabandeh in *A Muslim Commentary on the Universal Declaration of Human Rights* declares 'Anyone who penetrates beneath the surface to the inner essence of Islam is bound to recognize its superiority over other religions. A man, therefore, who deserts Islam, by that act betrays the fact that he must have played truant to its moral and spiritual truths in his heart earlier.' There can be no repentance for a Muslim who turns away from the Islamic Faith into which he was born. 'He is like a diseased member of the body politic, gangrenous, incurable, fit only for amputation and must be executed.', (F.T. Goulding, London, 1970) pp.71-2.

2.   A dreadful example of the refusal of the state to protect belief rights is to be seen in Iran where under Ayatollah Khomeini's leadership the Baha'i sect of 300,000 members have effectively been outlawed as heretics and become targets of Shiah Muslim fanatics. The Baha'i themselves are tolerant pacifists who respect all other religions, and especially Islam, as being inspired by God.

3.   Brownlie, *Basic Documents on Human Rights*, p.123.

4.   While it would not be unreasonable for the state to require that teaching in private religious schools should give factually adequate and accurate information about the wider world in which the religious sect exists, serious conflict will be avoided only if the state authorities approach this question sympathetically and if the religious school authorities are ready to accept that the wider society does have claims in this area.

5.   *Council of Europe: European Commission of Human Rights, Decisions and Report 19* (Strasburg, October 1980), *Pat Arrowsmith v. U.K.*

      In a dissenting opinion Mr Klecker argued that the pamphlet concerned should be considered as '*passive* encouragement in the sense that at no point does it openly advocate in strong terms that soldiers should desert or disobey orders.' (p.31).

It is difficult to see the force of E.M. Barendt's argument in '*Notes on Arrowsmith v. the U.K.*' that the distinction made by the Commission between expressing political opinion about the situation in Ireland and encouraging soldiers not to serve there or go absent without leave is 'a distinction without a real difference, reminiscent of the attempts of the Supreme Court to distinguish between the abstract advocacy of political doctrine and incitement to action.' Instead Barendt commends the distinction made by the Supreme Court in *Brandenberg v. Ohio*, 395.US. 44 (1969) between advocacy of law violation which is to be protected under the US First Amendment and the advocacy of imminent lawless action, likely to produce such action, which may be constitutionally prevented. This may be an appropriate standard for Western states to adopt, but not a standard which all states could be expected to apply. A case for even wider freedom of expression is made by T. Scanlon who argues that the notion of autonomous persons prohibits us from punishing anyone whose acts of expression lead other persons to commit harmful acts, 'where the connection between the acts of expression and the subsequent harmful acts consists merely in the fact that the act of expression led the agents to believe (or increased their tendency to believe) these acts to be worth performing.' 'A Theory of Expression', *Philosophy and Public Affairs*, Vol. 2 (Princeton University Press), reprinted in *The Philosophy of Law*, edited by R.M. Dworkin (Oxford University Press, 1977), p.161.

6.   These points were laid down by Trechsel for the European Commission on Human Rights in the *Handyside Case* before the European Court of Human Rights in *Publications of the European Court of Human Rights*, Series B, Vol. 22 (Strasburg, 1976), p.143.

The issue of pornography in relation to freedom of expression is discussed by Ronald Dworkin, 'Is There a Right to Pornography?', *Oxford Journal of Legal Studies*, Summer 1981, Vol. 2.

CHAPTER 5

1.   *The Nicomachean Ethics of Aristotle*, Bk IX, 1169b, edited by J.A. Smith, (J.M. Dent & Sons, Everyman Library), p.227.

2.   The problem of indigenous peoples is discussed by Professor Christian Bay, Toronto University, in an illuminating paper 'Post Liberal Citizenship, Human Rights and the Defence of Indigenous Peoples' submitted to the Twelfth World Congress of the International Political Science Association held in Rio de Janeiro, Brazil, in August 1982.

3.   I have discussed at some length the relationship between individual rights and the closed shop in Chapter 2 of *The Right to Strike* (Penguin Books, 1981).

4.   *European Court of Human Rights: Judgment in the Case of Young, James and Webster, 13 Jan. 1981* (Council of Europe, Strasbourg).

5.   Brownlie, *Basic Documents on Human Rights*, p.153. Article 1 states that 'the term "racial discrimination" shall mean any distinction, exclusion, restriction or preference based on race, colour, descent, or natural or ethnic origin which has the purpose or effect of nullifying or impairing the recognition, enjoyment or exercise, on an equal footing, of human rights and fundamental freedoms in the political, economic, social, cultural or any other field of public life'(ibid., p.151).

6.   *European Commission on Human Rights: Decisions and Reports, 18 July 1980. J. Glimmerveen and J. Hagenbeek v. the Netherlands, 11 October 1979* (Strasburg, 1980).

CHAPTER 6

1.   John Locke, *The First Treatise of Government* (section 42), from John Locke' *Two Treatises of Government*, Laslett edition (Cambridge, 1960). John Locke's theory of property has been the subject of extensive study. See in particular C.B. Macpherson, *The Political Theory of Possessive Individualism: Hobbes to Locke*, Ch. V (Oxford University Press, 1962) and James Tully, *A Discourse On Property: John Locke and his adversaries*, (Cambridge University Press, 1980).

2.   A third justification for private property is to be found in the theory of utility framed either in terms of economic efficiency or political and social stability. But there is an inherent tension between the notion of fundamental individual rights and the doctrine of general utility, (see Ronald Dworkin, *Taking Rights Seriously*), which makes it impossible to ground the former on the latter. A useful analysis of specific 'Arguments from Utility' is to be found in Lawrence C. Becker, *Property Rights: Philosophic Foundations* (Routledge & Kegan Paul, 1977).

3.   This is not perhaps as 'self-evident' a premise as it might seem, since one might accept that, as a last resort, a medical team would be justified in forcibly taking a pint of blood from a person of a rare blood group in order to save another's life.

4.   Richard E. Flatham, 'On the Alleged Impossibility of an Unqualified Disjustificatory Theory of Property Rights', in J. Roland Pennock and John W. Chapman, *Property: Nomos XXII* (New York University Press, 1980).

5.   J. Roland Pennock, 'Thoughts on the Rights to Private Property', ibid., pp.173-4.

6. Lawrence C. Becker, 'The Moral Basis of Property Rights', ibid., p.213.
7. It would follow from this that one cannot establish a fundamental human right either to dispose of property by testament or to inherit property through testament. Indeed one may go further and doubt whether one can legitimately speak of the rights of the dead and whether there can be any moral basis for a right of the dead to control the actions of the living. Neither the personality theory nor the labour theory can provide substantiation for a claim either of testamentary disposition or benefit. At most the former may provide a foundation for a claim of a general right of inheritance of purely personal effects.
8. Brownlie, *Basic Documents on Human Rights*, p.24.
9. Ibid., p.257.
10. Ibid., p.399.
11. The claim, if claim there be, would more appropriately be one of compensation for loss and injury, rather than of restitution. Such a claim would be substantiable by those small number of survivors from the terrible years of forced collectivization.

CHAPTER 7

1. It should be noted, however, that discussions of and demands for economic and social rights are not of recent origin. The seventeenth-century Leveller manifestos put forward a series of economic and social rights demands, as did Thomas Paine in *The Rights of Man* (Pt II, 1792).
2. General Assembly Resolution 32/130, 16 December 1977. *U.N. Chronicle*, No. 1, January 1978.
3. *Yearbook of the United Nations*, Vol. 32 (United Nations, 1978), p.712.
4. Maurice Cranston, *What Are Human Rights?* Ch. VIII, 'Economic and Social Rights' (The Bodley Head, 1973).
5. This matter is dealt with at some length in my book *The Right to Strike* (Penguin Books, 1981), Ch. 7, 'The Right to Strike as a Fundamental Human Right'.
6. Quoted in James Avery Joyce, *World Labour Rights and their Protection* (Croom Helm, 1980) p.64.
7. *National Union of Belgium Police Case, Public Hearings before the European Court of Human Rights (May 1975) Publications of the European Court of Human Rights, Series B, Vol. 17, 1973-75* (Strasbourg, 1976), p.235.
8. *Judgement of the European Court of Human Rights in the National Union of Belgium Police Case (27 October 1975), Publications of the European Court of Human Rights, Series A, Vol. 19* (Strasbourg, 1975), p.18. The Court reiterated this position in the *Swedish Engine Drivers' Union Case Judgement* of 6 February, 1976, adding that 'What the [European]

Convention [of Human Rights] requires is that under national law, trade unions should be enabled, in conditions not at variance with Article 11, to strive for their protection of their members' interest.' *Publications of the European Court of Human Rights, Series A, Vol. 20* (Strasbourg, 1976) pp.15-16.

9.   The European Social Charter came into force on 26 February 1965 and has been signed by eighteen members of the Council of Europe and ratified by thirteen. It requires all Contracting Parties to accept nineteen specific policy aims set out in Part I as follows: 1, the right to work; 2, the right to just conditions of work; 3, the right to safe and healthy working conditions; 4, the right to fair remuneration; 5, the right to organize; 6, the right to bargain collectively; 7, the right of children and young people to protection; 8, the right of employed women to protection; 9, the right to vocational guidance; 10, the right to vocational training; 11, the right to protection of health; 12, the right to social security; 13, the right to social and medical assistance; 14, the right to benefit from social welfare services; 15, the right of physically and mentally disabled persons to vocational training, rehabilitation and social resettlement; 16, the right of the family to social, legal and economic protection; 17, the right of mothers and children to social and economic protection; 18, the right to engage in a gainful occupation in the territory of other contracting parties; 19, the right of migrant workers and their families to protection and assistance.

Contracting parties undertake to be bound by at least five of the articles 1, 5, 6, 12, 13, 16, 19 and by a total of not less than ten articles (or forty-five numbered paragraphs of those articles). See Brownlie, *Basic Documents on Human Rights*, pp.301-18. Contracting parties submit bi-annual reports to the Secretary General of the Council of Europe and these reports are examined by a Committee of Experts appointed by the Committee of Ministers. The reports and conclusions of the Committee of Experts are submitted to a Sub-Committee of the Government Social Committee of the Council of Europe. That body reports to the Committee of Ministers which also receives the views of the Consultative Assembly on the Committee of Experts' conclusions. The Committee of Ministers may by a two-thirds majority make recommendations to the Contracting Party concerned. So far the Committee of Ministers has confined itself to drawing the attention of member parties to relevant Conclusions, Reports and Opinions. Paul Sieghart *The International Law of Human Rights* (Clarendon Press, Oxford, 1983) para. 32, pp.430-32.

10. Ibid., para. 24 3.4, pp.355-6.

11. Ibid., p.353.

12. Ibid., pp.357-8. See also Joyce, *World Labour Rights and their Protection* – Appendix B comprises ILO Convention 87 (1948) 'Concerning

Freedom of Association and Protection of the Right to Organize' and Convention 98 (1949) 'Concerning the Application of the Principles of the Right to Organize and to Bargain Collectively'.

13. ICES Article 8, 1(a), (c) and (d) respectively. Brownlie, *Basic Documents on Human Rights*, pp.120-21.

14. Ibid., p.119.

15. Quoted in 'Human Rights and Development: Working Papers No. 2', *Human Rights and the Basic Needs Strategy for Development*, by Philip Aston (Anti-Slavery Society, London, 1979) pp.26-7.

16. In *The Left and Rights* (Routledge and Kegan Paul, 1983) Tom Campbell argues that 'the socialist right to work,' as 'a right to have a satisfying part to play in a complex and changing pattern of inter-related production activities,' (p.184), is based on 'highly optimistic but it is hoped not outrageously Utopian assumptions about the feasibility of a model socialist society' (p.191).

17. In practice a significant part of the economy in all socialist states is in private hands, whether publicly recognized or encouraged (as with the collective farmers' private plots); accepted but frowned on (as with the 'fixers' who, at a price, help fill the gaps in the complex, inefficient state bureaucratic procurement machinery); or expressly forbidden and denounced (as when workers or managers use state materials and resources to fulfil private orders).

18. See *Five Constitutions: Contrasts and Comparisons*, edited and introduced by S.E. Finer, (Pelican Books, 1979) p.163. Article 40 guarantees the right to work.

19. See Amnesty, *Prisoners of Conscience in the USSR*, (Amnesty International, 2-edit 1980) pp.58-60.

20. *Cambridge Encyclopaedia of Russia and the Soviet Union* (Cambridge University Press, 1982) p.399.

21. European Social Charter, Article 1, Brownlie, *Basic Documents on Human Rights*, p.303.

22. Sieghart, *The International Law of Human Rights*, para. 18.1.3a, p.216.

23. Brownlie, *Basic Documents on Human Rights*, p.120.

24. Ibid., pp.303-4.

25. Sieghart, *The International Law of Human Rights*, para. 18.3.5, p.225.

26. Article 103 of ICES Rights states 'Children and young persons should be protected from economic and social exploitation. Their employment in work harmful to their morals or health or dangerous to life or likely to hamper their normal development should be punishable by law. States should also set age limits below which the paid employment of child labour should be punishable by law.' Brownlie, *Basic Documents on Human Rights*, p.121.

27. *The Anti-Slavery Reporter and Aborigine's Friend*, Series VI, Vol. 12,

No. 6, November 1979, published by the Anti-Slavery Society for Protection of Human Rights. It is worth noting that Columbia, India and Portugal have all signed and ratified ICES while Hong Kong as a British Crown Colony is not eligible to do so. Responsibility for the enactment and execution of legislation in Hong Kong is vested in a Legislative Council and Executive Council respectively, each consisting of officials and members appointed by the British Government.

28.   There is, for example, no justification for any state no matter how poor to tolerate child labour in the mines. The Anti-Slavery Society for the Protection of Human Rights Report on Columbia records that 'A recent report describes a coal-mine in which children work as deep as 280 m. underground in tunnels carved out of rock, the walls of which have no props. There is no ventilation, and the only light is provided by candles in cut-out tins on the side of the wall. There are no safety precautions. Children work eight hours a day, from 4 a.m. They hack the coal, fill the sacks and drag them up to the mouth of the pit; for each sack they earn about 7 pesos, and they will manage to fill about thirty during the day,' *The Anti-Slavery Reporter*, November 1979.

   ICES Article 103 states 'Children and young persons should be protected from economic and social exploitation. Their employment in work harmful to their morals or health or dangerous to life or likely to restrict their normal development should be punishable by law. States should also set age limits under which the paid employment of child labour should be prohibited or punishable by law'. Brownlie, *Basic Documents on Human Rights*, p.121.

29.   Brownlie, *Basic Documents on Human Rights*, p.122.
30.   Ibid., p.304.
31.   See I. Adelman and C.T. Morris, *Economic Growth and Social Equity in Developing Countries* (Stamford, USA, 1973) and Gerald M. Meier, *Leading Issues in Economic Development*, 3rd edition (Oxford University Press, New York, 1976) Section I, 'International Poverty and Inequality'. A major problem in making assessments in this area is the shortage of adequate reliable data.
32.   Brownlie, *Basic Documents on Human Rights*, p.121.
33.   Ibid., pp.307-9.
34.   European Code of Social Security and Protocol to the European Code of Social Security, *European Treaty Series No. 48 (1964)*.
35.   For details see European Convention of Human Rights, Sections II, III & IV, Brownlie, *Basic Documents on Human Rights*, pp.248-55.
36.   Brownlie, *Basic Documents on Human Rights*, Part Six Latin American Developments.
37.   Sieghart, *The International Law of Human Rights*, 19.0.3. p.239.
38.   Brownlie, *Basic Documents on Human Rights*, p.122.

39. Ibid., p.307.

40. David M. Smith, *Where the Grass is Greener: Living in an Unequal World* (Pelican Books, 1979). Table 5.1, p.249. Source, United Nations Research Institute for Social Development, 1976.

41. A 1966 survey in Uganda showed transport difficulties and costs resulted in out-patient attendances at hospitals falling from four to five visits a year for those living within two miles, to one visit for those between five and ten to twelve miles and once every ten years for those beyond that. With medical aid posts offering minimal treatment, visits halve with every additional mile of distance. Smith, ibid., p.283.

42. J.T. Hart, 'The Inverse Care Law,' *Lancet*, February 1971, quoted in Smith, ibid., p.261.

43. Smith, ibid., pp.34-8 and 264.

44. In 1971 the USA spent 7.4 per cent of its Gross National Product on health compared with 4.9 per cent in Britain. Ibid., p.258.

45. It should be noted, however, that although the United States of America signed both ICES and ICCPR on 7 October 1977 it has not ratified or acceded to either Covenant. The USA is, therefore, not a state party to either Convention. Ratification or accession would require approval by a two-thirds majority of the United States Senate.

46. Smith, *Where the Grass is Greener*, p.289.

47. ICES, Article 13.3, Brownlie, *Basic Documents on Human Rights*, p.123.

48. On the other hand there may be good grounds in developing countries for devoting resources to training medical assistants or 'bare-foot' doctors, able to provide basic treatment and to provide hygienic advice to the rural poor, rather than to turn out a small number of Western-style doctors, especially since the latter are more likely to serve the needs of the relatively affluent middle class. Positive discrimination in favour of selecting and training *native* 'bare-foot' doctors from among the peoples to be served may be conducive or even vital to the success of such an initiative.

49. Principle 7 of the 'Declaration of the Rights of the Child, 1959' states that the child should be given an education which will enable him 'on a basis of equal opportunity' to develop his abilities etc. (Brownlie, *Basic Documents on Human Rights*, pp.109-10); while Article 13.2(c) of ICES states that 'Higher education shall be made equally accessible to all on the basis of capacity.' (Ibid., p.123).

50. 'Reverse Discrimination', reprinted in Ronald Dworkin, *Taking Rights Seriously* (Duckworth, 1977).

51. A stimulating study of the problem to be found in Alan H. Goldman, *Justice and Reverse Discrimination* (Princeton University Press, New Jersey, U.S.A., 1979).

52. The International Convention on the Elimination of all Forms of Racial

Discrimination, 1966. Part I Article 1.4. reads:

> 'Special measures taken for the sole purpose of securing adequate advancement of certain racial or ethnic groups or individuals requiring such protection as may be necessary in order to ensure such groups or individuals equal enjoyment or exercise of human rights and fundamental freedoms shall not be deemed racial discrimination, provided, however, that such measures do not, as a consequence, lead to the maintenance of separate rights for different racial groups and that they shall not be continued after the objectives for which they were taken have been achieved.' Brownlie, *Basic Documents on Human Rights*, p.152.

53. Ibid., pp.122-3.
54. E. Durkheim, *Education and Society* (Free Press Glencoe, USA., 1956) p.71, quoted in David Lane, *Politics and Society in the USSR* (Weidenfeld & Nicholson, 1972), p.486.

CHAPTER 8

1. Brownlie, *Basic Documents on Human Rights*, p.118 and pp.128-9. The European Convention on Human Rights does not guarantee the right to self-determination.
2. Ibid., pp.28-9.
3. Sieghart, *The International Law of Human Rights*, para. 26.1 p.369.
4. Lung-Chu Chen, 'Self-determination as a human right', in *Towards World Order and Human Dignity: Essays in Honor of Myres S. McDougal* (The Free Press, New York) 1976, pp.216 and 243.
5. A good example of this is to be seen in Spain where the new democratic Spanish state has accorded important regional rights to the peoples in the Basque Province, with the approval of the overwhelming majority of the Basque people. This has led the Basque terrorist organization ETA to wage an indefensible campaign of terrorism to secure through force an independence which the Basque people have themselves rejected.
6. 'U.N. Convention on the Prevention and Punishment of the Crime of Genocide' (1948), Brownlie, *Basic Documents on Human Rights*, p.31.
7. The allusion is to the oft-quoted distinction made by Marx in the concluding passage to *The Poverty of Philosophy* (1847) between the early stage of capitalism where the mass of workers constitute a class 'for itself' with objective interests opposed to that of the capitalist class, and the latter stage when through its experience of struggle against the capitalists 'this mass becomes united, and constitutes itself as a class in

itself.' Quoted in Robert C. Tucker, *The Marx-Engels Reader* (2nd Edition, 1978), p.218.

8. Resolution 32/152 of the United Nations General Assembly, 16 December 1977, *UN Chronicle*, January 1978.

9. Resolution 36/133 of the United Nations General Assembly, 14 December 1981, *UN Chronicle*, March 1982.

10. ICPR and ICES both include the following Articles:

'All peoples may for their own ends, freely dispose of their natural wealth and resources without prejudice to any obligations arising out of international economic cooperation, based upon the principle of material benefit and international law. In no case may a people be deprived of its own means of subsistence.' (Article 1(2) in both Covenants).

'Nothing in the present Covenant shall be interpreted as impairing the inherent right of all peoples to enjoy and utilize fully and freely their natural wealth and resources', ICPR (Article 47), ICES (Article 25).

11. Quoted in introduction to Kamal Hossain (ed.), *Legal Aspects of the New International Economic Order* (Frances Pinter for the Centre for Research on the New Economic Order, 1980).

The Charter of Economic Rights and Duties of States (Note 4, Art.2 (2)c) also provides under the principle of permanent sovereignty over natural resources for the right of any state

'to nationalize, expropriate or transfer ownership of foreign property, in which case appropriate compensation should be paid by the state adopting such measures, taking into account the relevant laws and regulations and all circumstances that the state considers pertinent. In any case where the question of compensation gives rise to controversy, it shall be settled under the domestic law of the nationalizing state and its tribunals, unless it is freely and mutually agreed by all the states concerned that other peaceful means be sought on the basis of the sovereign equality of states and in accordance with the principle of free choice of means.'

General Assembly Resolution 3281, 29 United Nations General Assembly, 1974.

12. Professor W.H. Balekjian, *Report of the 60th Conference of the International Law Association, Montreal 1981* (International Law Association, 1983), p.235.

13. The International Bill of Human Rights refers to the rights set forth in the United Nations Declaration of Human Rights, plus the two International Covenants (ICES and ICPR plus Optional Protocol).

14. *United Nations Economic and Social Council (E/CN4/1334) 2 January 1979. Commission on Human Rights, 35th Session. Report of the Secretary-General.*

15.   Theodoor Van Boven, 'Recent Events Mark a Link between Human Rights and the New International Economic Order,' *UN Chronicle*, August 1980.

16.   Karel de Vey Mestdagh, 'The Right to Development', *Netherlands International Law Review*, 1981, pp.47-53.

17.   *Report of the 60th Conference of the International Law Association*, (Montreal 1981), p.232.

18.   Norwegian Agency for International Development (NORAD), *Norway's Economic Relations with Developing Countries* (2nd Edition, Oslo, 1977). Quoted by United Nations Secretary General in Report to United Nations Economic and Social Council, *Commission on Human Rights, 35th Session*, para. 269-70.

19.   *General Assembly Resolution 32/130, 16 December 1977.*

20.   *Puritanism and Liberty, Being the Army Debates (1647-9) from the Clarke Manuscripts with Supplementary Documents*, selected and edited with an introduction by A.S.P. Woodhouse (J.M. Dent & Sons, 1938), p.63.

21.   William Cobbett from *Advice to Young Men and Women, Advice to a Citizen* (1829) quoted in Michael Oakeshott, *The Social and Political Doctrines of Contemporary Europe* (Cambridge University Press, New York, 1950), p.30.

22.   See ibid., pp.30-32 and Tom Paine, *Dissertation on First Principles of Government* (R. Carlisle, 1819), pp.11-15.

23.   See Sieghart, *The International Law of Human Rights*, para 25.0.4 p.363.

24.   In 1976 three patients at a Cheshire Mental Hospital won an appeal against having their names deleted from the electoral register. Geoffrey Alderman, *British Elections: Myth and Reality* (Batsford, 1978), p.43.

25.   John Stuart Mill, *Representative Government* (1861), Ch. VIII, 'Of the Extension of the Franchise'.

26.   See Sieghart, *The International Law of Human Rights*, 25.0.5, pp.364-5.

27.   It is possible, however, to use an election for purposes other than those for which it was called. Thus the Sinn Fein MPs elected at the British General Election of 1918 refused to go to Westminster but instead met as the first Irish Dail and proclaimed Irish independence.

28.   The classification used here derived from the studies in *Elections Without Choice*, edited by G. Hermet, R. Rose and A. Rouquié (Macmillan, 1978).

29.   Brownlie, *Basic Documents on Human Rights*, p.136.

30.   Ibid., p.136.

31.   Ibid., p.25.

CHAPTER 9

1. United Nations Universal Declaration of Human Rights, Article 1, 1948.
2. See for example the wide-ranging collection of texts published by UNESCO as a special contribution to International Human Rights Year, 1968, entitled *The Birthright of Man*.
3. United Nations Charter Articles 2.1 and 2.7, Brownlie, *Basic Documents on Human Rights*, p.4. The Human Rights Committee of the United Nations set up under the International Covenant on Civil and Political Rights may only receive complaints by one state party against another where both are parties to that Covenant and both recognize the competence of the Committee to consider complaints. The Committee has no enforcement powers but makes 'its good offices' available to those states which specifically recognize under Article 41 'the competence of the Committee to receive and consider communications to the effect that a State Party claims that another State Party is not fulfilling its obligations under the present Covenant'. Under the Optional Protocol of ICCPR the Human Rights Committee may consider communications from individuals in states party to the Optional Protocol who claim to be victims of violations by their own state of the Covenant on Civil and Political Rights. The Committee makes its views known to the State Party concerned and to the individual. In both cases the Committee examines communications in closed sessions. By 1 January 1982, sixty-nine states had ratified ICPR but only fourteen had made a declaration under Article 14 and only twenty-seven had signed the Optional Protocol.
4. The Chief Justice of Tanzania in an address to a Conference of Judges and Magistrates in Dar-es-Salem in 1965 stated:

> First of all, the One-Party state here is very different from that in the communist or fascist setting – the difference lies not only in the constitution but in the philosophical basis of the Single Party. Communism or fascism as political doctrines deal with the entirety of human behaviour, including the field of legal theory and, while there may not be an absence of legality, quite often legal processes are inverted to serve other ends. This is clearly not the case here. There has been no explicit founding of the One-Party state on any identifiable political theory. This means that there is no pattern of legal thinking to which the judicial officer is obliged to conform – no party line on jurisprudence.

Printed in *Human Rights in a One-Party State; International Seminar on Human Rights, Their Protection and the Rule of Law in a One-Party*

State, convened by the International Commission of Jurists (Search Press London, 1978), p.54.

5. The Preamble of the Universal Declaration of Human Rights declares 'whereas it is essential, if man is not to be compelled to have recourse, as a last resort, to rebellion against tyranny and oppression, that human rights should be protected by the rule of law'. Brownlie, *Basic Documents on Human Rights*, pp.21-2.

6. Convention on the Prevention and Punishment of the Crime of Homicide, Articles IV, VIII & IX, ibid., p.32.

7. I propose to carry out research into these issues under the auspices of the United Nations University.

8. Brownlie, *Basic Documents on Human Rights*, p.136.

9. *Human Rights in a One-Party State*, p.85.

10. Brownlie, *Basic Documents on Human Rights*, p.118 & p.128.

11. See Resolution 37/100c of the General Assembly of the United Nations 2nd Special Disarmament Session of 13 December 1982 which called on Member States 'to facilitate the flow of accurate information on disarmament to and among their citizens and to encourage their citizens freely and publicly to express their own views on disarmament questions and to organize and meet publicly for that purpose' (adopted without a vote). The Assembly also requested the Committee on Disarmament 'to undertake negotiations on an international convention prohibiting the use or threat of use of nuclear weapons under any circumstances'. (Resolution 37/100c, adopted by 117 to 17 with 8 abstentions.

12. *Nuclear War: The Aftermath*. A special AMB 10 publication published under the auspices of the Royal Swedish Academy of Sciences (1983) estimates 750 million deaths outright from a major nuclear war involving the use of less than half the explosive power in the Soviet and American nuclear arsenals.

Index

DATE DUE

MAY 2 7 1993			

DEMCO 38-297